I STILL BELIEVE
ANITA HILL

THREE GENERATIONS DISCUSS THE LEGACIES
OF SPEAKING TRUTH TO POWER

EDITED BY **AMY RICHARDS** AND **CYNTHIA GREENBERG**

THE FEMINIST PRESS
AT THE CITY UNIVERSITY OF NEW YORK
NEW YORK CITY

Published in 2013 by the Feminist Press
at the City University of New York
The Graduate Center
365 Fifth Avenue, Suite 5406
New York, NY 10016

feministpress.org

First printing January 2013

Cover design by Herb Thornby, herbthornby.com
Text design by Drew Stevens

Library of Congress Cataloging-in-Publication Data
I still believe Anita Hill / edited by Amy Richards and Cynthia Greenberg.
    p. cm.
  ISBN 978-1-55861-809-1
1. Hill, Anita. 2. Sexual harassment of women--United States. 3. Feminism
—United States. I. Richards, Amy, 1970– II. Greenberg, Cynthia.
HQ1237.5.U6I22 2012
305.42—dc23
                                                    2012031114

For Anita Hill
With courage and conviction,
you changed the world.

CONTENTS

PART II. RESPONDERS: WHAT DOES ANITA HILL MEAN TO YOU?

APPENDIX

EDITORS' NOTE

Most of the text included in this collection was verbally delivered on Saturday, October 15, 2011, at a conference commemorating the twentieth anniversary of Anita Hill's testimony. The conference, Sex, Power, and Speaking Truth: Anita Hill 20 Years Later, was organized around five main discussions and this book includes all of them. Two sections, originally presented as a conversation, have been adapted here as essays. Performance pieces from the sold-out evening event, curated by Eve Ensler and Purva Panday Cullman, are woven throughout the book. Here is a note from Eve Ensler and Purva Panday Cullman about the evening performances:

> When we were asked to curate an evening performance to honor Anita Hill, the first question we asked ourselves was *What does it mean to speak truth to power?* Our intention was to create an evening that would include a collage of diverse voices that not only honored Anita Hill's great courage in speaking the truth in the face of such scrutiny, but also presented our audience

with a renewed call to action to seek justice for women in the workplace, the courtroom, the classroom, and beyond. It was an electric night, charged with an excitement and sense of urgency that only the theater can create.

An archive of the conference's proceedings can be found at anitahill20.org.

EXCERPTS FROM THE TESTIMONY OF ANITA HILL AT THE CLARENCE THOMAS SENATE CONFIRMATION HEARINGS, OCTOBER 11, 1991

Senator Howell Heflin (D-Alabama): Are you a scorned woman?

Anita Hill: No.

Senator Howell Heflin: Are you a zealot civil rights believer?

Anita Hill: No, I do not have that kind of complex. I do not like all of the attention that I am getting.

Senator Arlen Spector (R-Pennsylvania): Do you have anything to gain by coming here? Has anyone promised you anything by coming forth with this story now?

Anita Hill: I have not gained anything, except knowing that I came forward and did what I felt that I had an obligation to do, and that was to tell the truth. . . . After approximately 3 months of working [with Thomas at the Department of Education], he asked me to go out socially with him. What happened next and telling the world about it are the two most difficult things, experiences of my life. It is only after a great deal of agonizing consideration and a number of sleepless nights that I am able to talk of these unpleasant matters to anyone but my close friends . . .

I declined the invitation to go out socially with him, and explained to him that I thought it would jeopardize what at

the time I considered to be a very good working relationship
. . . I believed then, as now, that having a social relationship
with a person who was supervising my work would be
ill advised. I was very uncomfortable with the idea and told
him so.

I thought that by saying "no" and explaining my reasons,
my employer would abandon his social suggestions. However,
to my regret, in the following few weeks he continued to
ask me out on several occasions. He pressed me to justify
my reasons for saying "no" to him. These incidents took
place in his office or mine. They were in the form of private
conversations, which would not have been overheard by
anyone else . . .

My working relationship became even more strained
when Judge Thomas began to use work situations to discuss
sex . . .

He spoke about acts that he had seen in pornographic
films involving such matters as women having sex with
animals, and films showing group sex or rape scenes. He
talked about pornographic materials depicting individuals
with large penises, or large breasts, individuals in various
sex acts.

On several occasions Thomas told me graphically of his
own sexual prowess. Because I was extremely uncomfortable
talking about sex with him at all, and particularly in such
a graphic way, I told him that I did not want to talk about
these subjects. I would also try to change the subject to
education matters or to nonsexual personal matters, such as
his background or his beliefs. My efforts to change subject
were rarely successful . . .

The comments were random, and ranged from pressing me about why I didn't go out with him, to remarks about my personal appearance. I remember him saying that someday I would have to tell him the real reason that I wouldn't go out with him.

He began to show displeasure in his tone and voice and his demeanor in his continued pressure for an explanation. He commented on what I was wearing in terms of whether it made me more or less sexually attractive . . .

When I informed him that I was leaving [my job], I recall that his response was that now I would no longer have an excuse for not going out with him. I told him that I still preferred not to do so . . .

[When I left my job] . . . he made a comment that I will vividly remember. He said that if I ever told anyone of his behavior that it would ruin his career. This was not an apology, nor was it an explanation.

See appendix for additional excerpts from Anita Hill's testimony.

WHEN YOU SPEAK UP

EVE ENSLER

When you stand,
when you speak up
speak back
speak out,
when your voice trembles
throat chokes,
brow sweats
when you can't walk away
can't sleep
can't pretend
it didn't happen,
doesn't matter
when you were taught all along
to be polite
to not make a fuss
not put yourself in the center of things
when it's so obvious
so unjust
so crazy wrong

you can't imagine anyone
could disagree
when you have to say
have to go
have to fight.
When they come at you
from unpredictable directions
with every menacing tool
when they instinctively know
your Achilles' heel
or pay researchers to find it.
When they don't say directly
we are practiced sex harassers
we don't want black people here
we think women should be seen not heard
when they say instead
you're a lousy teacher
a scorned woman
narcissistic egocentric
sophomoric writer
got hired on affirmative action
a hack,
a whore.
It doesn't require tougher skin.
It requires the suspension of skin
when nothing in your training
prepared you
to be hated
despised
misinterpreted

misunderstood
undermined
reduced
shamed
dark hole
when you fall into it.
When you tell yourself
it isn't fair
your life is hard
you already suffered enough.
It's true.
When you tell yourself
you didn't choose it
yes you did.
When the group you love
more than your life
calls you Judas
and turns on you.
When the dark hole
suddenly grows spikes
remember your heart
is a piñata
you don't get the gifts
'til its smashed open.
When you suddenly get hit
with issues you never knew
were issues
which are not really issues
except those in power
have made them seem like issues—

you didn't come forward before
you went back to the room
you called him again.
Power under attack
is genius at diversion.
They have PhDs in it.
When you want to withdraw
deeper into the hole.
When all the voices blur
and its somehow the same voice
that told you once
you were stupid
selfish
wrong
and you're suddenly five
and thirty five
exiled then
and now.
When hate shrapnel's in your mouth
your stomach
your soul.

When you're on your knees screaming out
when the pain is so intense
it takes you somewhere else
it takes you out of you
no one can touch you there.
You will never be afraid like that again.

And women will know
it is possible
it is possible
it is possible.

EVE ENSLER is a Tony award-winning playwright, performer, and activist. She is the author of *The Vagina Monologues*, which has been published in forty-eight languages and performed in over one hundred and forty countries. Ensler's newest work, *I Am An Emotional Creature: The Secret Life of Girls Around The World*, was published in book form, and made the *New York Times* best-seller list. The play, *Emotional Creature*, was made into workshops in Johannesburg, South Africa and Paris, France. It opened at Berkeley Repertory Theatre in June 2012, and opens in New York in November 2012. She is also the founder of V-Day, the global movement to end violence against women and girls, which has raised over 90 million dollars. Ensler's play *Here* was filmed live by Sky Television in London, UK. Her other plays include *Necessary Targets*, *The Treatment*, and *The Good Body*, which she performed on Broadway, followed by a national tour. In 2006, Ensler released her book, *Insecure At Last: A Political Memoir*, and co-edited *A Memory, A Monologue, A Rant and A Prayer*. She is currently writing a new book, *In the Body of the World*.

INTRODUCTION

In the fall of 1991, I was a young, impressionable college student, feeling the righteousness of my age and era. Like many others I was stopped in my tracks when I watched what unfolded one October day: an all white Senate Judiciary Committee grilling and humiliating a black woman who was subpoenaed to come before them to offer testimony into Clarence Thomas's character as he was being considered for a Supreme Court nomination.

Twenty years later, under the guidance of a small, but hearty, organizing committee we created a commemorative conference, which took place on October 15, 2011, at Hunter College. Nineteen years previously Hunter had hosted a similarly themed conference, where thousands came to vent and heal from what had happened that previous year. I was not in attendance, but I was part of that group determined not to let history repeat itself. Within a year of these hearings I co-founded the Third Wave Foundation. As was the case for so many others, the hearings were my last straw, the moment I realized that I had a responsibility to start enacting my vision for a just society.

Twenty years later, Clarence Thomas is still a Supreme Court justice and Anita Hill is a tenured professor at Brandeis University. Instances of assaults on women—by politicians, by law enforcement, by their lovers, by their families—persist. In their homes, in their workplaces, in the military, on the street, no woman is free from gender-based violences.

When we came together to show solidarity for Anita so many echoed "I could have been Anita." We came together to show that no woman is alone, to affirm that the women's movement is a mighty force, and to prove that—given purpose and conviction—we will move justice forward.

—Amy Richards

A COMMENT, NOT CASUAL, CONCERNING ANITA HILL

MARY OLIVER

If we're moving anywhere toward a goal of a more ethical world, universally and solidly, it's often difficult to be persuaded that it's happening. What will help? Thoughtfulness, of course, and action. Thoughtfulness is the result of reflection within ourselves; action is something more. It needs a truly stout heart. We learn about it frequently from those who before us have insisted upon some small or large demonstration; thus may the rest of us feel the aura of courage.

Anita Hill, twenty years ago, could have kept silent. Very few people, in general, will thank you for rocking the boat. Instead: the finger pointing, questioning, chiding, blaming, and endless media exposure. Who will choose this? Anita Hill chose it, and thus she is a light to all of us. So determined that the truth should be heard! Anita Hill acted in those difficult days with grace, integrity, and a lot of grit. Not without cost to herself surely. Viktor Frankel wrote somewhere, "What is to give light must endure burning." Yes, that's the way it is. All the same, Anita Hill came forward; we owe her our praise and our thanks.

MARY OLIVER, born in a small town in Ohio, published her first book of poetry *No Voyage and Other Poems* in 1963 at the age of twenty-eight. She has since published many works of poetry and prose. The *New York Times* recently acknowledged Oliver as "far and away, this country's best-selling poet." Over the course of her long and illustrious career, she has received numerous awards. Her fourth book, *American Primitive*, won the Pulitzer Prize for poetry in 1984. Oliver was editor of *Best American Essays 2009*. She currently lives in Provincetown, Massachusetts, the inspiration for much of her work.

PART I

WITNESSES: WHAT HAPPENED?

REMEMBRANCES: THE ANITA HILL HEARINGS— TWENTY YEARS LATER

LOUISE M. SLAUGHTER
MAUREEN DOWD
PATRICIA SCHROEDER

Louise M. Slaughter:

The battle to let Anita Hill's voice be heard will always be one of the most important battles I've ever fought, and one of the seminal moments of my time in the United States Congress.

Throughout the hearings, our approach to a mountain of opposition was simple: we just wouldn't accept it. In addition to our many meetings demanding that Anita Hill be allowed to speak, our small group of outraged congresswomen stayed at the Senate Judiciary Committee throughout, listening to every minute of the hearing, our intentions clear. We were going to make sure that Anita Hill's story was told.

I look back with mixed emotions upon one of the most important events in modern American history. The indifference that many of our male colleagues in the House and Senate showed toward Ms. Hill was a microcosm of the way women were being treated all across our country. Women were being shown what happens to you if you speak up against male superiors, and the attempts by many of our male colleagues to silence Anita Hill were reprehensible.

Yet, the grassroots uprising that the hearings sparked among American women was a great step forward for women, and a turning point in American culture. The hearing was a key moment when American women joined together to demand equality. The victory that American women achieved that day is something that has always stuck with me, especially when it comes to fighting for women's freedoms, rights, and equality.

One of the most important things we can do is to teach our children and grandchildren about the tremendous levels of indifference and discrimination women faced just twenty years ago, and the need to always be our fiercest advocates.

Maureen Dowd:

The Anita Hill hearings were the most searing professional experience of my life, like a psychic dentist's drill sinking into the most sensitive, least explored parts of the national consciousness on sex, race and power.

My friend Ruth Marcus of the *Washington Post* has said that everyone in the Senate Judiciary hearing room that week couldn't wait for it to be over.

I felt the reverse. I wanted it to go on longer, until the web of lies Clarence Thomas wove with such bravado was torn away. I kept waking up in the middle of the night trying to figure out what had really happened between these two intense, accomplished people. Any rush to justice might mean a justice on the Supreme Court who had used the Big Lie and lynching imagery to cow a bunch of white, male senators.

I remember chasing Arlen Specter down the hall to ask how he could vilify Hill as a bitter perjurer? I remember feeling outraged when Joe Biden, the chairman of the committee, cut the hearing short before calling the two women who could have testified to Thomas's unseemly intimidation of women in the office. I remember feeling disheartened that Edward Kennedy, muted by his own reputation with women, could not combat Orrin Hatch's absurd contention that Thomas, an aficionado of X-rated films, was an altar boy who could not possibly know the language of pornography. I still remember Clarence Thomas with his hand on a Bible ascending to the Supreme Court for life.

Patricia Schroeder:

In 1991, when I was co-chair of the congresswoman's caucus, I organized a few of us to make one-minute speeches at the opening of the congressional session about our great, so-called liberal leaders on the Senate Judiciary Committee. These guys just didn't get it. They were ignoring sexual harassment allegations against Clarence Thomas, and they didn't want Anita Hill to testify.

When we women finished our speeches, we realized the Senate Democrats were meeting that day for policy discussions so we decided to march over to the Senate and talk to them in person. March we did! You may remember seeing front-page pictures of us striding up the steps of the building. We knocked firmly on the door. Majority Leader George Mitchell opened it.

"Sorry," he said "We don't let strangers into our meetings."

STRANGERS! We were dumbfounded but we had the presence of mind to point out that a huge press corps was following us. Mitchell quickly agreed to meet with us later in his office and there, he agreed to pressure the committee into letting Anita Hill testify.

Chairman Biden grudgingly put her on the witness list but *not* in prime time. He also rejected the other women who stepped forward as witnesses. It was painful to watch the Democratic senators on the Judiciary Committee—those cowardly lions—quiver and quake. They were pitiful, and no help at all.

Anita Hill knew the real Clarence Thomas. Anita Hill warned the nation about him. Sadly, those who could have done something to prevent his joining the Supreme Court did not listen because in their eyes, women's claims of sexual harassment had no gravitas.

Anita Hill, you are, and will always be, my hero!

Congresswoman **LOUISE M. SLAUGHTER** represents the twenty-eighth Congressional District of New York State. Slaughter is the ranking member of the influential Committee on Rules and the first woman to serve as its chair. A member of the House Democratic Leadership, she also serves on the prestigious Democratic Steering and Policy Committee.

MAUREEN DOWD is a renowned columnist for the *New York Times* and best-selling author of *Bushworld: Enter at Your Own Risk* and *Are Men Necessary?: When Sexes Collide*. She began at the *Times* in 1983 as a metropolitan reporter; prior she worked at *Time* magazine and the *Washington Star*. She was awarded the Pulitzer Prize for her series of columns on the Clinton administration and the Monica Lewinsky scandal.

PATRICIA SCHROEDER is a former congresswoman from Colorado, and author of two books, *Champion of the Great American Family* and *24 Years of Housework and the Place Is Still a Mess: My Life in Politics*. Retiring from over twenty years of public service in 1997, which included service on the Judiciary Committee and co-founding the Congressional Woman's Caucus, Schroeder taught at Princeton University's Woodrow Wilson School of Public and International Affairs, and then served as President and CEO of the Association of American Publishers. She currently chairs the English Speaking Union, and is vice chair of the Marguerite Casey Foundation.

A THANK YOU NOTE TO ANITA HILL

LETTY COTTIN POGREBIN

I want to personally thank you, Anita Hill, for what you did for us twenty years ago. Thank you for speaking up and speaking out. Thank you for your quiet dignity, your eloquence and elegance, your grace under pressure. Thank you for illuminating the complexities of female powerlessness, and for explaining why you didn't complain when the offense first occurred, and for describing how cowed and coerced a woman can feel when she is hit on by a man who controls her economic destiny.

Twenty years ago you had the courage to tell the truth and do what women rarely did: Make a scene. Fifty years ago I didn't.

In the 1960s, when I was a book publishing executive, single, and self-supporting, I was once trapped in an elevator with a powerful male journalist whose good offices I depended upon to give favorable coverage to my company's books. With absolutely no warning, the man suddenly pinned me against the elevator wall, groped my breasts, and shoved a hand under my skirt. Did I press the emergency button?

Of course not. It would have caused a scene. A scene would have imperiled my career. A scene would have marked me as a prude, a troublemaker, and that grimmest of all characters, A Girl With No Sense of Humor. A scene would have infuriated and embarrassed the man. A scene might have made the newspapers, exposing his crude and thuggish behavior to his wife. In the end, the person who would pay a price for his humiliation would be me. He would bad-mouth me in the industry. He would give my company bad press, which in turn would reflect badly on my work and put my job at risk.

That's why, instead of screaming and pressing the emergency button, I giggled while I fought him off. I spewed wisecracks as I twisted out of his grasp. I tried to keep smiling while frantically stabbing the "L" button. Finally, the elevator doors opened on the lobby floor and I made a run for the street.

It wasn't the first or the last time that I escaped an unwanted sexual advance and ended up feeling sullied, scared, cowardly, and somehow at fault. Far worse happened to friends of mine and to hundreds of thousands of working women in even more difficult financial circumstances.

But thanks to you, Anita, we and our daughters and granddaughters now feel empowered to press the emergency button and report offensive behavior. Thanks to your brave, frank testimony and your stately comportment in the face of hostile interrogation and vilification by members of the Senate Judiciary Committee, we no longer laugh off unwanted sexual advances; we file charges. We no longer protect our attackers from humiliation; we name names. We demand that our employers stand accountable to their published policies against harassment and that the offender be punished. We may still be risking our jobs, but more and more of us are telling the truth.

It all started with you, Anita. We honor you for what you did.

We thank you for making a scene—for doing it fearlessly before the eyes of a riveted nation, and thus inspiring millions of women to defend their dignity as you did yours.

LETTY COTTIN POGREBIN, co-chair of the Sex, Power, and Speaking Truth: Anita Hill 20 Years Later conference, is a writer, lecturer, and social justice activist with a special interest in women's issues and the Israeli-Palestinian conflict. A founding editor of *Ms.* magazine, Pogrebin is the author of ten books, including the novel, *Three Daughters*, and two acclaimed memoirs, *Getting Over Getting Older*, and *Deborah, Golda, and Me: Being Female and Jewish in America*. Her latest nonfiction work is *How To Be A Friend To A Friend Who's Sick* (forthcoming). She was the editor of *Stories for Free Children*, a book based on the monthly feature of the same name in *Ms.*, and was the editorial consultant on *Free to Be You and Me*, the groundbreaking children's multimedia project created by Marlo Thomas. Pogrebin served four years as President of the Authors Guild, and two terms as president of Americans for Peace Now (APN). Pogrebin's many honors include annual listings in *Who's Who in America*, the Yale University Poynter Fellowship in Journalism, a Matrix Award from Women in Communications, an Emmy Award (for her contributions to *Free to Be You and Me*), and the Distinguished Alumni Award from Brandeis University.

TWENTY YEARS LATER

DOROTHY SAMUELS

The weekend of the Thomas-Hill hearings and the political maneuvering that surrounded them quite literally stopped the nation.

Testifying before the all-male Senate Judiciary Committee, Anita Hill told in frank detail of being subjected to vulgar sexual advances by President George H. W. Bush's nominee to the Supreme Court, while she worked for him a decade earlier at two government agencies. Her account, and Clarence Thomas's angry if unforthcoming response had Americans glued to their TV screens. It was soap opera, and a riveting social, legal, and political history lesson all rolled into one.

Across the country, in offices, homes, universities restaurants, and on street corners, people talked of nothing else. The ensuing debate over who was telling the truth and whether such behavior by a Supreme Court nominee, if it occurred, should defeat a president's choice for the nation's highest court, at once divided and united the nation.

Suddenly, thanks to this mass consciousness-raising exercise, the issue of sexual harassment was out of the shadows. And we have been seeing and feeling and living the ripples ever since.

For Professor Hill's courage and her grace and perseverance under unimaginable pressure, all Americans, and women especially, owe her a tremendous debt of gratitude.

What follows is a distinguished group of individuals, some of whom had direct personal involvement in the events that transpired on Capitol Hill twenty years ago, and all of whom have valuable experiences and insights to share which can help us understand what happened in the Hill-Thomas drama and why it still matters today.

DOROTHY SAMUELS has been a member of the *New York Times* editorial board since 1984, where she writes on a wide array of legal and social policy issues. Prior to joining the *Times*, she briefly practiced corporate law with a big Wall Street firm, but left to pursue her interests in public policy and journalism. For four years, Samuels served as executive director of the New York Civil Liberties Union, the largest affiliate of the national ACLU. In 2001, in a change of pace, she published a comic novel, *Filthy Rich*.

ANITA HILL: STILL SPEAKING TRUTH TO POWER TWENTY YEARS LATER

CHARLES OGLETREE

When Anita Hill went to testify in Washington, DC in October 1991, she spoke truth to power. And it may be that for a moment power prevailed. But, in reality, the truth finally is upon us. The women's movement stood firmly behind Professor Hill, and twenty years later we can celebrate the power of truth!

Before I address the issues of sexual harassment, I want to acknowledge a warrior we recently lost in the struggle for gender equality. He was with us twenty years ago, and, his spirit is with us today. My mentor, hero, and teacher, Professor Derrick Bell passed away on October 5, 2011. If Derrick were alive today, he'd be in the back row, not the front, cheering on women saying, "We have to equalize society if we're ever going to make progress." Thank you, Derrick, for standing up.

To give you a context about the magnitude of this loss, as we celebrate the landmark stance by Professor Hill in 1991, we must remember Derrick Bell was always a progressive. He was the first African American with tenure at Harvard Law School, but then left the school because Harvard didn't tenure more people of color. He went to the University of Oregon, and became the first African American dean of a major American university. He left there in 1985 because they refused to give an Asian American woman tenure. He came back to Harvard. A few black men were there when he returned, including me, but Harvard had not hired a woman of color to its tenure track faculty. In 1990, Professor Bell, defiant as always, took a stand, speaking truth to power, when he proclaimed: "Unless Harvard hires a woman of color on the tenure track, I'm leaving." After that proclamation, hundreds of students were in front of a rally at Harvard on the campus in 1990 and Derrick Bell was about to speak. He was introduced that day by a skinny kid who was a second-year law student at Harvard Law School, and the president of *Harvard Law Review*. His name was Barack Obama. Obama talked about Bell's contribution to diversity. The most important thing he said in introducing Professor Bell in 1990: Derrick Bell was the Rosa Parks of the legal profession. Think about that. Barrack Obama was well informed about the future as well as the past.

It became even more interesting a year later. I'm minding my own business, not tenured yet at Harvard Law School, and I get a call to come assist Professor Hill. I was happy to do that and to assist the volunteer team of lawyers and supporters in the preparation for her appearance before the United States Senate Judiciary Committee, then composed of over a dozen white men, Democrats and Republicans. After what I thought was a productive preparation session, I returned to my hotel room for a short nap before departing early the next morning to return to Cambridge. I had planned to get an early morning flight because I had to complete writing and editing a law review article that would ultimately become a part of my tenure package. At about 6:00 a.m. on an October morning in 1991, two women knocked

fact finder. "You can't be a prosecutor and the judge. You have to be clear on your role as a senator. Decide your role." Apparently, he did not appreciate my claim. At the end of the hearing, he refused to even shake my hand.

Every night at midnight or one o'clock I would call my wife and family to report what was going on. One night I called home and my twelve-year-old daughter, Rashida, came on the phone and she said, "Dad, I've been watching the hearings. I want you to know I believe Anita Hill." To make that come full circle, Rashida went on to NYU Law School, where she was a Root-Tilden-Kern Public Interest Fellow. And she was taught by and served as a teaching assistant for none other than Derrick Bell. Two generations of Ogletree's were fortunate to be taught by Professor Derrick Bell.

What's important to remember is that Professor Hill stood up for others, not just for herself. That puts her in a class with Susan B. Anthony, Rosa Parks, Fanny Lou Hamer who said, "I'm sick and tired of being sick and tired." With Eleanor Roosevelt, Hillary Clinton, my grandmother, my mother, my aunts, my daughter, my three granddaughters, who are growing up in a world where they know they are and can be the best possible they can be and neither gender nor race will be a barrier because they know that they can overcome. Because Anita Hill stood up for the rights of women in 1991, we can all stand up to salute her in 2011.

CHARLES OGLETREE is the Jesse Climenko Professor of Law at Harvard Law School, and founding and executive director of the Charles Hamilton Houston Institute for Race and Justice. Ogletree's most recent book is *The Presumption of Guilt: The Arrest of Henry Louis Gates, Jr.* and *Race,*

Class and Crime in America. He has published (with Austin Sarat) *From Lynch Mobs to the Killing State: Race and the Death Penalty in America; When Law Fails: Making Sense of Miscarriages of Justice;* and *The Road to Abolition: The Future of Capital Punishment in the United States.* In 2009 Ogletree was awarded the prestigious American Bar Association Spirit of Excellence Award. In 2008, the *National Law Journal* named Ogletree one of the 50 Most Influential Minority Lawyers in America, and he has been named as one of the 100 Most Influential Black Americans by *Ebony* magazine for the past six years.

BUT SOME OF US ARE BRAVE

LANI GUINIER

I start with a confession. Clarence Thomas and I were friends in law school. It was not surprising, since he and I were two of very few black students in our 1L class. We both wanted to become civil rights lawyers. Because of my ties to the NAACP Legal Defense Fund (LDF),[1] I was able to help Clarence get his first summer job working with an integrated law firm in Savannah.

In the Spring of 1973, Clarence and I had driven to Philadelphia from New Haven so we could hear Elaine Jones, a brilliant LDF attorney, give a mesmerizing speech about the civil rights cases on which she was working. LDF represented black applicants trying to gain admission to the state bars throughout the South. By then Clarence had told me that he wanted to go back to Savannah "and work for a black law firm handling civil rights

---

1. The summer after my first year in law school I had worked for Chambers, Stein, Ferguson and Becton, the first integrated law firm in North Carolina. The lawyers at the firm had a close relationship with the NAACP LDF national office. One of the partners, Julius Chambers, later became director-counsel of the LDF.

cases."[2] At his request, I helped him raise the money that enabled him to spend the summer between his second and third years of law school working at the law firm Hill, Jones and Farrington in Savannah.[3] In his memoir, Clarence describes Bobby Hill, one of the firm's named partners—and one of the few black elected officials in the Georgia State legislature—as "flamboyant, brilliant and courageous."[4] During the time Clarence worked in Savannah that summer, I interned at LDF, assisting Elaine Jones on the bar discrimination cases she was pursuing throughout the South.

I spent most of my time that summer in the LDF New York office doing what I loved: researching, writing, and strategizing with Elaine about her active cases. The highlight of the summer, however, was Elaine's invitation to become an "eyewitness to injustice." She asked me to fly from New York to Alabama to take notes during her deposition of an official of the Alabama state bar. Elaine had found out that at various points in its recent history, the Alabama state bar had required those who wanted to be admitted to the bar to submit a photograph in order to sit for the bar examination. Although the requirement was formally "neutral," it had predictable effects. It helped explain why, on the list of the bar applicants, some applicants' names were preceded by the letters "col." I don't recall Elaine questioning the official directly as to the reasons a photograph was required. Instead I watched as Elaine approached the issue in her own distinctive way. She raised her voice an octave or so to broadcast

2. Clarence Thomas, *My Grandfather's Son: A Memoir* (New York: Harper, 2007), 79–80.

3. Ibid., 81. Eventually, Clarence got a sixty-dollar-a-week grant from a fund supported by LDF (matched by forty dollars a week from the law firm Hill, Jones and Farrington).

4. Ibid. As Clarence writes in his memoir, one of the lawyers at the firm, Bobby Hill, was also a member of the Georgia legislature.

her indignation. "Why" she asked, "were the letters 'c,' 'o,' and 'l,' followed by a period, on the application roster next to some of the applicants' names?" "Oh," the official blithely replied. "They must have been colonels in the army!" I was speechless.[5]

When Clarence and I returned to Yale in the fall of 1973, he listened attentively to my stories and shared some of his own. We seemed to be on the same page; indeed, we contemplated the possibility of writing a law review article together, reflecting our joint concern regarding the low bar passage rates for black applicants in the South. After all, both Clarence and I, at that time, wanted to become civil rights lawyers. And in Clarence's case he intended to take the Georgia bar, which, by then, was also the subject of a civil rights lawsuit alleging that the Georgia bar's administration practices were racially discriminatory.[6]

In the end, Clarence chose another road. As a result, we didn't see each other much after law school. And then, eighteen years later, I watched on television as Clarence testified before a committee of the United States Senate, on his way to becoming a justice of the United States Supreme Court.

In 1973, I had witnessed an official with the Alabama state bar squirm as Elaine Jones questioned him about the letters "c," "o," "l," followed by a period, next to the names of bar exam applicants. This was *witnessing as discovery*. In 1991, however, the act of bearing witness was different than it was in 1973. Watching the hearings in 1991 was *witnessing as theater*.

---

5. It is true that "col" may be shorthand for a senior commissioned officer in the military. But it was truly unexpected to learn that an Alabama official would boldly attempt to deflect Elaine's questions by hypothesizing that it was men of rank (not men of "color") who were flagged and thus among those most likely to fail the bar.

6. See Cecil Hunt, "Guests in Another's House: An Analysis of Racially Discriminatory Bar Performance," *Florida State University Law Review* 23 (1996): 721, 734.

The Hill-Thomas hearings were, in fact, spellbinding. In some ways they were a throwback to the early 1950s, a period when seeing a black person on television, even for a few seconds, was an event. Back then, if the TV camera flashed on a black person, my husband Nolan, then a child, would shout to his older brother Milton, "Come quick Milton. There's a Negro on TV!" His brother would stop whatever he was doing and race to bear witness. Yet, no matter how quickly Milton bounded into the room, the fleeting image of the Negro invariably was gone. Although the image was no longer visible, the fact of its presence nevertheless served as a form of acknowledgment. Negroes were people after all.

Like the fleeting image of a Negro on TV in the early 1950s, the confirmation hearings were an event to be witnessed. This time, Nolan and I were able to sit in our Philadelphia home and view living, breathing black professionals for broad stretches of time on television. We not only saw the witnesses; we could also hear them speak. Nevertheless, the black witnesses were instructed to play a limited role. They were there to speak politely, and to answer only those questions posed by the senators, all of whom were white and male.

The act of witnessing the Hill-Thomas hearings thus felt oddly voyeuristic. Anita Hill, like Clarence and me, had been a student at Yale Law School at a time when black women were still a tiny numerical minority. During this period, women of all colors were not only a minority; they were also mostly silent. We rarely talked about what we saw during the day. If it came up at all, it was under cover of darkness or as a secret, whispered only to each other. Despite our collective silence in public, or perhaps because of it, we had bonded. Yet now, a decade or so later, there were still very few women's voices at the hearings. We were still mainly whispering to each other. But one woman's soft spoken voice made it through. It was the voice of Anita Hill.

Dayna Cunningham, a very good friend and one time colleague at the LDF, remembers with vivid specificity the phone call she got on the first day of Anita Hill's testimony. When the phone rang, Dayna did not know who was calling. The caller did not ask, "how are you?" He did not give his name. Instead of greeting her like the friend he was, he skipped the conventional pleasantries and got right to the point of his call. "Are you black or are you a woman?" he asked Dayna. "Tell me!" he commanded. "Are you black or are you a woman?"

The question had real power as did the demand for an immediate answer. Its power arose from an implicit ultimatum for racial unity. Racial unity, in his eyes, was a necessary part of the act of bearing witness. Both the listener and the questioner were forcefully propelled to engage directly with the claim that a person of color cannot have multiple identities. Despite the ultimatum, and because of what she was witnessing in the Hill-Thomas proceedings, Dayna suddenly could see the futility of the demand that we choose between gender and race. Whether as women or as persons of color, we did not have a singular identity.

Dayna was not alone in her refusal to accommodate the demand for a singular identity. Other women of color gradually came to a similar understanding. Their identity as "both/and" had started slowly but eventually snowballed as black women like Dayna began to bear *public* witness to a new understanding of ourselves. This new understanding was spurred both because of and in response to the Thomas confirmation hearings. Enabled by important scholarship on intersectionality and the multiple ways that race and gender converge or overlap, what had been a closeted conversation became a public dialogue of continuing significance.[7] Yes, we said to one another. Yes, it was possible to be both black and a woman (in real life *and* on television).

The post-hearing debate spawned a new era; the 1990s became a decade of women bearing witness. We witnessed and ultimately participated in a long-term debate provoked by—but not discussed at—the hearings themselves. It was a debate that mostly took place *outside* of the Senate hearing room. It was a debate that was propelled by phone conversations and public discussions that continued long after Senator Biden gaveled the hearings to a close. It was not, as in the mainstream media, a debate about which witness was telling the truth. Instead, it was a collective culture-shifting moment that occurred simultaneously on television and offstage within the black community. It was a debate within the black community about what it means to be both black and a woman.

The post-hearing debate surfaced the need for a new meaning to the act of bearing witness. Bearing witness helped inspire complex black political resistance to the idea that there is any single understanding of what it means to be a black woman in America. Bearing witness ushered in a new phase of black women's consciousness of power. Attempts to enforce racial solidarity created the groundwork for racial complexity.

At the same time, the act of witnessing the hearings helped change the face of power itself. Initially, during those hearings, it appeared that power rested with the senators, all of whom

7. See, e.g., Kimberlé Crenshaw, "Mapping the Margins: Intersectionality, Identity Politics, and Violence Against Women of Color," *Stanford Law Review* 43 (1991): 1241–99; Audre Lord, "When I dare to be powerful, to use my strength in the service of my vision, then it becomes less and less important whether I am afraid." *The Cancer Journals*, Special Edition (San Francisco: Aunt Lute Books, 1997), 13.

were white, all of whom were male. However, the act of bearing witness in 1991 helped many of us begin to appreciate the poignancy of a collection of essays edited in 1982. The subtitle of that book of essays is *All the Women are White, All the Blacks are Men*. The title is *But Some of Us Are Brave*.[8]

While the subtitle was the implicit premise of my friend Dayna's telephone interlocutor, it was the title—*But Some of Us Are Brave*—that spoke to the testimony of Anita Hill. It was a tribute to Anita Hill's stoic audacity; at the same time it was a call to arms. For many women of color, the subtitle and the title captured the importance of bearing witness as well as the complexity of opinion and of position within our shared fate.

Some of us were in the Senate hearing room. Some of us were in our own living rooms. Most importantly, we were all present. We were transfixed by the moment that eventually became a legacy. And over time our sense of ourselves changed.

After all, what we witnessed was not merely a conflicting set of perspectives involving two people. What we witnessed over time was a paradigm shift, "the embodiment of things hoped for, but yet unseen."[9] Surely Dayna's interlocutor was wrong. We bore common witness and ultimately began to experience a collective awakening. We discovered a common truth: All the women are not white, all the blacks are not men, and some of us, especially when we organize and work together, are very brave.

8. Patricia Hill Collins, Gloria Hull, and Barbara Smith, eds., *But Some Of Us Are Brave: All the Women Are White, All the Blacks Are Men* (New York: The Feminist Press, 1982). See, e.g., xxiv and xxviii: "As Black women we belong to two groups that have been defined as congenitally inferior in intellect, that is Black people and women. . . . This book is, in essence, the embodiment of things hoped for, yet unseen."
9. Ibid.

LANI GUINIER was the first woman of color appointed to a tenured professorship at Harvard Law School and is now the Bennett Boskey Professor of Law. Before her Harvard appointment, she was a tenured professor at the University of Pennsylvania Law School. Guinier worked in the civil rights division at the US Department of Justice and then headed the voting rights project at the NAACP Legal Defense Fund in the 1980s. Guinier has published many scholarly articles and books, including *The Tyranny of the Majority*; *Becoming Gentlemen: Women, Law School, and Institutional Change* (with co-authors Michelle Fine and Jane Balin); *The Miner's Canary: Enlisting Race, Resisting Power, Transforming Democracy* (co-authored with Gerald Torres); and *The Tyranny of the Meritocracy: How Wealth Became Merit, Class Became Race and Higher Education Became a Gift From the Poor to the Rich* (forthcoming).

OLD AND NEW DEPICTIONS OF JUSTICE: REFLECTIONS, CIRCA 2011, ON HILL-THOMAS

JUDITH RESNIK[1]

W hat does one need to know now about what happened twenty years ago? The frame for my answers comes from Toni Morrison, writing in 1992, and wisely advising:

> For insight into the complicated and complicating events that the confirmation of Clarence Thomas became, one needs perspective, not attitudes; context, not anecdotes; analyses, not postures. For any kind of lasting illumination, the focus must be on the history routinely ignored or played down or unknown.[2]

1. Arthur Liman Professor of Law, Yale Law School. All rights reserved, October, 2012. My thanks to those who brought the 2011 commemoration activities into being, to Anita Hill, and to John Frank whom, as Anita remarked in her comments at the conference producing this volume, paved the way in the 1950s and 1960s as an exemplar of a lawyer and law professor committed to the fair treatment of all persons both before the law, in classrooms and in his office. This chapter, completed with the thoughtful help of Ester Murdukhayeva, Edwina Clarke, and Elizabeth Wilkins, when students at Yale Law School, builds on my own work in 1991 on behalf of Anita Hill, on essays I have written about those events, and on the book, co-authored with Dennis Curtis, entitled *Representing Justice: Invention, Controversy and Rights in City-States and Democratic Courtrooms* (New Haven, CT: Yale University Press, 2011), which is the source for some of the historical materials and imagery referenced here.
2. Toni Morrison, "Introduction: Friday on the Potomac" in *Race-Ing Justice, En-Gendering Power: Essays on Anita Hill, Clarence Thomas, and the Construction of Social Reality* (New York: Pantheon, 1992), xi.

My focus is on four facets of that "history"—about what happened before, when, and after Anita Hill made her public statements—that need to be inscribed.

A first piece of the "history routinely ignored" is the set of exchanges during the week before the Senate Judiciary Committee re-convened to address Hill's information. On October 6 and 7, 1991, the press reported that Anita Hill had come forth with allegations of sexual harassment by Thomas, who had been her boss when he chaired the Equal Employment Opportunity Commission (EEOC).[3] At that time, Anita Hill's name was not well-known. Many responded with apparent disinterest. The confirmation vote was scheduled for October 8. The conventional wisdom was that Thomas's confirmation was a fait accompli and would become official, given the fifty-eight senators planning to vote for him.

But a remarkable number of people around the United States disagreed with the idea of ignoring Hill's claims and felt a need to do something—and many did. Within ten hours, one hundred and twenty women law professors (myself included) had signed a letter, sent to the Senate Judiciary Committee, calling for a full inquiry into what had transpired.[4] By the next day, October 8, the newspapers ran a picture of seven women—all members of the US House of Representatives—marching up the steps of the Capitol to ask that the Senate delay the vote.[5]

3. Neil A. Lewis, "Law Professor Accuses Thomas of Sexual Harassment in 1980s," *New York Times*, October 7, 1991, A1.

4. Letter from women law professors to the Senate, October 7, 1991, also referenced in Maureen Dowd, "The Thomas Nomination: The Senate and Sexism," *New York Times*, October 8, 1991, A1, col. 4.

5. Maureen Dowd, "The Thomas Nomination: 7 Congresswomen March to the Senate to Demand Delay in Thomas Vote," *New York Times*, October 9, 1991, A1, col. 4. The members of Congress were: Barbara Boxer (California); Nita M. Lowey (New York); Patsy T. Mink (Hawaii); Eleanor Holmes Norton (nonvoting delegate,

The uproar stopped the process but only for one week, and the official request for the delay came from Senator Danforth on behalf of Clarence Thomas.[6] The Senate Judiciary Committee announced it would hold a hearing on October 11, 1991, which fell that year on the eve of Columbus Day weekend.[7] And thus, on that Friday, Anita Hill went before the Senate and via television before the world.

Why remember this fragment about timing? How does it provide perspective, give context, and yield analysis? The brief respite captured both women's newfound power and its limits. The Senate's initial disinterest in Anita Hill's information was a vivid reminder that not long before, disinterest in women's rights of all kinds was the norm.

Given how commonplace concerns about women's equality and the term "sexual harassment" have become, it may be difficult to appreciate that before the 1970s, no one had even asked nominees to the Supreme Court anything about their attitudes toward women's rights.[8] Moreover, before the 1970s, the Supreme Court had not interpreted the Fourteenth Amendment of the United States Constitution to protect women against

District of Columbia); Patricia Schroeder (Colorado); Louise Slaughter (New York); and Jolene Unsoeld (Washington).

6. Edwin Chen and Paul Houston, "Senate Delays Vote on Thomas to Probe Harassment Charges," *Los Angeles Times*, October 9, 1991.

7. Holding the hearing on that Friday provided one of the references to the Friday of Morrison's essay, "Friday on the Potomac," see note 2. The other "Friday" that Morrison invoked is the character Friday in Daniel Defoe's novel, *Robinson Crusoe*. Morrison pointed to poignant parallels between Thomas and Friday, losing their own voices to mimic master and collaborating with authorities against others like themselves.

8. See Judith Resnik, "Judicial Selection and Democratic Theory: Demand, Supply and Life Tenure," *Cardozo Law Review* 26 (2005): 579, 631–34; Judith Resnik, "Changing Criteria for Judging Judges," *Northwestern University Law Review* 84 (1990): 889, 893–96.

gender-based discrimination.[9] Not until 1986 did the Supreme Court hold that sexual harassment at work constituted a violation of the federal law (Title VII of the 1964 Civil Rights Act) prohibiting work-place discrimination based on race, religion, ethnicity, and sex.[10]

Of course, women knew well about their own unequal treatment. The specific issue of sexual harassment was familiar to many women who faced harassment in workplaces, in their homes, and in the streets. Yet, until pathbreaking work (including that of many writing in this volume[11]), women's lack of ownership over their bodies was just the way it was.

Yet just as collective action on October 8, 1991 produced a pause in the Thomas confirmation process, collective action during the 1970s and 1980s produced Anita Hill's ability to name "sexual harassment" as wrong. Sets of practices once tolerated as "just the way it was" came to be understood as legally repressible wrongs—sexual harassment, date rape, gender-based discrimination, and subordination.

The transformation resulted from the work of women and men who linked so-called "private" moments of discomfort, distress, and terror to discrete political and legal wrongs. As one recalls (or sees fresh by watching the video of the 1991 confirmation questioning), one needs to appreciate that the effort to disparage Anita Hill was a form of a (sad) victory, encoded in the obnoxious behavior that ensued. Once, such allegations

9. The first Supreme Court decision addressing sex-based discrimination was Reed v. Reed, 404 US 71 (1971) (holding that an Idaho probate law that gave men preference over women in appointing administrators of estates was an unconstitutional violation of the Equal Protection Clause).

10. Meritor Savings Bank v. Vinson, 477 US 57 (1986).

11. See, e.g., Catharine MacKinnon, *Sexual Harassment of Working Women: A Case of Sex Discrimination* (New Haven, CT: Yale University Press, 1979).

would simply have been dismissed, and no hearing would have been held. Once, some men (raced, classed) assumed they could exercise that form of privilege over women's bodies or that such actions were not so improper as to be the subject of an inquiry. But by 1991, winks and nods no longer sufficed. Rather, the defense had to be that no harassment had happened and/or that whatever had transpired was the fault of the woman.

In short, a context in which to place the Hill-Thomas exchanges is inside the social movements that made the initial decision of the Senate Judiciary Committee to ignore the allegations politically untenable. The legal, cultural, and political work of several decades had not only made women into rights-holders but had also changed the meaning of what constituted a right—and a wrong.

The second context for the events of October 1991 requires that the clock be rolled back again, this time to the summer of 1991, so as to remember another piece of history that is also at risk of being forgotten. Opposition to the confirmation of Clarence Thomas came long before the information provided by Anita Hill. Clarence Thomas had taken a number of stances—against affirmative action, against abortion, against state-provision of assistance[12]—that were contrary to the views of many civil

---

12. See, e.g., Clarence Thomas, "Affirmative Action: Cure or Contradiction?" *Center Magazine* 21 (November/December 1987); Clarence Thomas, "Affirmative Action Goals and Timetables: Too Tough? Not Tough Enough!" *Yale Law and Public Policy Review* 5 (1987): 402, 404 [hereinafter Thomas, Affirmative Action Goals]; Clarence Thomas, "Rewards Belong to Those Who Labor," *Washington Times*, January 18, 1988; Clarence Thomas, "The Higher Law Background," *Harvard Journal of Law and Public Policy* 12 (1989): 63–64. Thomas's anti-abortion stance was inferred from his discussion of natural law and passing references to *Roe v. Wade*. See David Savage, "Thomas Hearings Likely to Focus on Abortion Issue," *Los Angeles Times*, July 14, 1991.

rights proponents and organizations, and several came forth during the first phase of the Thomas hearings to object.[13]

For example, while chairing the EEOC, Thomas had cut back on the enforcement of the Equal Pay Act and had narrowly interpreted aspects of Title VII.[14] Moreover, Thomas rejected what then the Supreme Court had approved (what he termed "numerical remedies"), and argued that

> distributing opportunities on the basis of race or gender, whoever the beneficiaries, turns the law against employment discrimination on its head. Class preferences are an affront to the rights and dignity of individuals—both those individuals who

13. Nomination of Judge Clarence Thomas to Be Associate Justice of the Supreme Court of the United States, Hearings before the Committee on the Judiciary, US Senate, 102d Cong., 1st Sess. 127 (Sep. 10–13, 16–17, 19–20 and Oct. 11–13, 1991) [hereinafter Thomas Hearings]. Witnesses testifying that the nomination should not be confirmed included Drew Days (Yale Law School), Christopher Edley Jr. (Harvard Law School) and Charles Lawrence (Stanford Law School) testifying on behalf of the Society of American Law Teachers, Thomas Hearings Part II, 2–30; William H. Brown and Erwin N. Griswold, testifying on behalf of the Lawyers Committee on Civil Rights Under Law, Thomas Hearings Part II, 96–143; Kate Michelman of the National Abortion Action League, Thomas Hearings Part II, 526–31; Faye Wattleton, Planned Parenthood Federation of America, Thomas Hearings Part II, 531–42; Representative John Conyers, Congressional Black Caucus, Thomas Hearings Part II, 667–74; Harriet Woods, National Women's Political Caucus, Thomas Hearings Part III, 200–01; Molly Yard, National Organization for Women, Thomas Hearings Part III, 202–05, and Anne Bryant, American Association of University Women, Thomas Hearings Part III, 232–39. A minority of two members of an ABA Committee also concluded that Thomas was not qualified for the role, while a majority found him to be qualified. See Testimony of Ronald Olson, Chair, Standing Committee on the Federal Judiciary, American Bar Association, Thomas Hearings, Part I, 523 and 532.

14. During Thomas's tenure at EEOC, the number of Equal Pay Act cases dropped significantly. While the agency filed fifty cases in 1980, it filed fewer than ten in several years of Thomas's chairmanship, including a low of five cases in 1988. See Women Employed Institute, *EEOC Enforcement Statistics* (1991). Similarly, the number of class action lawsuits fell from 218 in 1980 to 128 in 1989, the final year of Thomas's chairmanship (Ibid). Thomas explained the reduction in class action suits because he believed the "emphasis on 'systemic suits led the Commission to overlook many of the individuals who came . . . to file charges and seek assistance." Thomas, Affirmative Action Goals, 404.

are directly disadvantaged by them, and those who are their supposed beneficiaries. I think that preferential hiring on the basis of race or gender will increase racial divisiveness, disempower women and minorities by fostering the notion that they are permanently disabled and in need of handouts, and delay the day when skin color and gender are truly the least important things about a person in the employment.[15]

In addition, when giving speeches, Thomas had singled out abortion rights for criticism.[16] And, when interviewed in the press, Thomas had commented on his sister's receipt of federal benefits when she was out of work.[17]

Yet various civil rights groups that had raised concerns about other nominees hesitated to do so about Thomas. The many muted voices reflected the mixed emotions evoked when confronting any presidential nominee and especially a black man named to fill a seat held by Thurgood Marshall, the first and only other African American to sit on the United States Supreme Court.

Nonetheless, several important critiques were made—all before the events encapsulated in "Hill-Thomas." Two eloquent examples come from Professors Kim Crenshaw (also writing

15. Thomas, Affirmative Action Goals, 403.

16. See, e.g., Clarence Thomas, "Why Black Americans Should Look to Conservative Policies," The Heritage Foundation Lecture 119 (June 18, 1987): 8.

17. Thomas was quoted as saying that his sister got "mad when the mailman was late with her welfare check." The comment was reported by Juan Williams, "Black Conservatives, Center Stage," *Washington Post*, December 16, 1980, A21. See Neil A. Lewis, "Thomas's Journey on Path of Self-Help," *New York Times*, July 7, 1991, also quoted in Testimony of Patricia King, Professor, Georgetown University Law Center (September 17, 1991), Thomas Hearings, Part II, 269 [hereinafter King Testimony, Thomas Hearings]. See also Karen Tumulty, "Sister of High Court Nominee Traveled Different Road," *Los Angeles Times*, July 5, 1991, A4. At the hearings, Thomas stated he had "no recollection of ever making a statement about my sister in any speeches. That was in one news article on December 16, 1981." Thomas Hearings, Part IV, 248.

in this volume) and Patricia King, both of whom believed that
Thomas's record made him ill-suited to sit on the Supreme
Court.[18] Professor King, who testified in September of 1991
before the Senate Judiciary Committee, explained that in light of
Judge Thomas's "extensive record and personal posture [being]
so antithetical to the interests of women and blacks—especially
black women," she felt obliged to record her opposition to the
nomination.[19] Professor King explained that Judge Thomas had
"repeatedly attacked well-established Supreme Court case law
on affirmative action" and, that when chairing the EEOC, he
had "deliberately chose[n] not to seek goals and timetables" for
remedies, and reduced the "number of class action cases filed,"
despite their utility for Title VII cases.[20]

Professor King also raised concerns about Thomas's public
criticism of his sister as a recipient of public benefits for a time.
As King explained, Thomas's sister had married, had children,
and supported them "by holding down two minimum wage jobs"
before leaving (and later returning to) the wage workforce to
take care of their aunt who had become ill.[21] King detailed how
"African-American women [were] four times as likely to be low
wage workers" than white women. King drew the lesson that
Thomas's sister provided a model of the "ethos of family support,
resourcefulness, and interdependence" of black women, as well

18. See Kimberlé Crenshaw, "Roundtable: Doubting Thomas," *Tikkun* 6 (September–October 1991): 23, 27–28. She explained: "My sense of Clarence Thomas is that he doesn't represent the much-heralded phenomenon of pulling oneself up by one's bootstraps. The story instead is how he climbed over the body of his sister and metaphorically the bodies of the very Black women he insults with his willingness to demean us for his own political gain."

19. King Testimony, Thomas Hearings, 266–75.

20. Ibid., 272.

21. Ibid., 271–73.

as an exemplar of the very limited opportunities faced by single heads of households.[22]

The third context in which to search for more of what Toni Morrison called "lasting illumination" comes from honing in on the process provided by the Senate Judiciary Committee in October of 1991 and then widening the lens to consider the treatment of women in court-like settings more generally. At the 1991 hearing, some senators repeatedly invoked a trial-like stance, with mentions of "burden of proof" as they claimed they had devised procedures to provide "fairness."[23] But their format revealed the proceeding to be what Dennis Curtis later called it—a "fake trial."[24]

Five days to prepare was only one of the problems, and the repeated renegotiation of the rules of the proceeding was another. Moreover, although the senators were to be the judges of the relevance of the information, many senators acted like prosecutors, casting Anita Hill in the role of defendant. At the same time, some also took on a role akin to that of defense counsel for Thomas. They aggressively interrogated Hill and discounted her responses. Further, the Judiciary Committee declined to invite other testimony, including from an academic expert prepared to explain the challenges of raising harassment claims and from another witness coming forth to describe her own experiences with Thomas.[25]

22. Ibid.

23. See David G. Savage, "Thomas, Backers Try to Make Him Seem Victim," *Los Angeles Times*, October 13, 1991, A1, col. 3. Savage quoted Senator Joseph Biden: "The presumption (of innocence) remains with you, judge."

24. See Dennis E. Curtis, "The Fake Trial," *Southern California Law Review* 65 (1992): 1523.

25. See, e.g., Kim A. Taylor, "Invisible Woman: Reflections on the Clarence Thomas Confirmation Hearing," *Stanford Law Review* 45 (1993): 443, 447; Louise F. Fitzgerald, "Science v. Myth: The Failure of Reason in the Clarence Thomas Hearings," *Southern California Law Review* 65 (1992): 1399, 1400.

What people watching television saw was a young black woman being badgered and a black man awkwardly questioned by the fourteen white men then comprising the Senate Judiciary Committee. An uproar ensued, as many people got it—that race, gender, and ethnicity were playing roles affecting the inquiry and undermining the fairness of the decision-making procedures.

The Senate proceedings did more, for they provided a glimpse into what happened, sometimes, in real courts. The exchanges in the Senate put faces on justice— and what it looked like, with slight modification, mirrored the reality of state and federal courthouses around the country. Anita Hill and Clarence Thomas were not the only disputants encountering authorities who looked different from them. In federal and state courts in that decade, the judges were mostly men, and almost all were white. Litigants were—and are—far more diverse. One thus gained insight into far more ordinary occurrences, through looking at the extraordinary exchanges in the Senate.[26]

Moreover, in the 1970s and 1980s, as women and men went to state and federal courts and made arguments about forms of discrimination, they encountered some judges, some juries, and

26. To be specific, in 1990, about seven hundred and forty people sat as life-tenured federal trial judges and, at that time, 7 percent (or forty-nine) were women. Around then, fewer than 9 percent were judges of color. See Administrative Office of the US Courts, Annual Report of the Judicial Equal Employment Opportunity Program for the Twelve-Month Period Ended September 30, 1990, 8, tbl. 1. The two categories—"women" and "men"—without mention of race or gender reflect that until 1993, the United States courts did not focus on data reflecting intersectionality. Instead, the data on federal judicial branch employees described them either as women or men, or as "white, black, Hispanic, Asian, American Indian, and handicapped."

The state courts looked similar—in 1991, about 9 percent of the twenty-eight thousand state judges were women, and one can only find intersections by looking state by state. Florida recorded about 1 percent of its judges then as women of color. Report and Recommendations of the Florida Supreme Court Racial and Ethnic Bias Study Commission 2, 1990, 49–60.

some prosecutors who shared the very stereotypes on display in the Hill-Thomas exchanges. And just as in Hill-Thomas, many organizations came together in an effort to intervene in the unfairness that they saw.

In 1980, the NOW Legal Defense and Education Fund created a National Judicial Education Program and, joined by the National Association of Women Judges, pressed the leaders of courts to take up the question of their own procedures. In 1982, the chief judge of New Jersey led the way by chartering a "gender bias task force." In 1985, New Jersey led the way again by chartering a "minority concerns task force."[27] In 1997, New Jersey was once again first when the state's chief justice chartered a task force on sexual orientation and the courts.[28]

By the early 1990s, when Anita Hill and Clarence Thomas testified, more than thirty jurisdictions had issued reports on gender and race and ethnic bias. Many of the reports documented the challenges of being a witness, seen vividly in the questioning of Anita Hill. Indeed, in 1986, New York State's Task Force on Women in the Courts concluded that:

> Cultural stereotypes of women's role in marriage and society daily distort courts' application of substantive law. Women uniquely, disproportionately, and with unacceptable frequency

27. New Jersey Supreme Court Task Force on Women in the Courts, First Report, June 1984 (detailing the history); New Jersey Supreme Court Task Force on Minority Concerns, Final Report, June 1992.

28. See New Jersey Supreme Court, Final Report of the Task Force on Sexual Orientation, January, 2001. See generally Lynn Hecht Schafran, "Gender Bias in the Courts: An Emerging Focus for Judicial Reform," *Arizona State Law Review* 21 (1989): 237; Vicki C. Jackson, "What Judges Can Learn From Gender Bias Task Force Studies," *Judicature* 81 (1997): 15; Judith Resnik, "Asking About Gender in Courts," *Signs* 21 (1996): 952.

must endure a climate of condescension, indifference and hostility.[29]

New York's Task Force on Minorities issued its findings in 1991, the same year in which Thomas was nominated. That study reported:

> the numerous complaints, testimony and comments received by the Commission reflect the perception that minorities are stripped of their human dignity, their individuality and their identity in their encounters with the court system.[30]

Neither state report was unique; many volumes, officially commissioned by state chief justices or state bars, detailed the specific challenges of encounters framed by gender, race, and ethnicity.[31] In response to such inquiries, many courts around the country changed their rules and procedures so as to insist on dignified and equal treatment of women and men of all colors. Educational programs for lawyers and judges focused on gender and racial bias in the courts. New codes of conduct for lawyers and judges were put into place. In a few, rare cases, trial judges who permitted mistreatment or themselves mistreated women and men of color were reversed on the grounds that their behavior was impermissibly biased.[32]

29. See Report of the New York Task Force on Women in the Courts 5, 1986. See also Judith Resnik, "From the Senate Judiciary Committee to the County Courthouse: The Relevance of Gender, Race, and Ethnicity to Adjudication," in *Race, Gender, and Power in America: The Legacy of the Hill-Thomas Hearings,* ed. Anita Faye Hill and Emma Coleman Jordan (New York: Oxford University Press, 1995) 177, 181–97.

30. See Report of the New York State Judicial Commission on Minorities, The Public, and The Courts, Vol. II, 1, 1991.

31. See Resnik, "Asking About Gender," 953–54.

32. See, e.g., Catchpole v. Brannon, 36 Cal. App. 4th 237 (1995). Maria Catchpole

Some jurisdictions also looked at how to diversify their benches. For example, Florida's task forces generated concern about judicial selection and helped prompt legislation obliging that selection committees include women and/or minorities. And while that distinction (women and/or minority) sits uncomfortably with those attentive to intersectionality (in what category do women of color fall?), the statute had an impact when it was in effect; the more diverse selection committee yielded more diverse results.[33]

But some of these efforts were met with objections—that raising questions of unfairness based on gender, race, and ethnicity inscribed such problems. Opponents of affirmative action criticized task forces as undermining the color-blind attitude that they advocated for judges and for legal doctrine. The Supreme Court held illegal some affirmative action programs developed for workplaces and thereafter, the Florida statute was struck down on federal constitutional grounds—as unlawful affirmative action.[34] Furthermore, in the mid-1990s, a few senators called for government investigations into task forces convened to consider the effects of gender and race in the federal courts. In short, the conflict over what constituted fair treatment for Hill and for Thomas in the Senate has been replayed in courthouses around the United States as well as in the Congress.

---

had alleged that she had been subject to sexual harassment while employed by a restaurant. See Sheri Lynn Johnson, "The Color of Truth: Race and the Assessment of Credibility," 1 MICHIGAN JOURNAL OF RACE AND LAW 261(1996); see also Jeffrey J. Rachlinski, Sheri Lynn Johnson, Andrew J. Wistrich, and Chris Guthrie, "Does Unconscious Racial Bias Affect Trial Judges?," Notre Dame Law Review 84 (2009): 1195.

33. See FLA. STAT ANN. § 43.29 (West Supp. 1993) (requiring that one of the three members of the panels proposing judges be "a member of a racial or ethnic minority or a woman"). See also Resnik, "Asking About Gender," 959.

34. See Mallory v. Harkness, 895 F. Supp. 1556 (S.D. Fla. 1995).

A fourth slice of courthouse history (falling under Toni Morrison's category of "history that is not known") is needed as a predicate to my conclusion. In the 1930s, in the wake of the Depression, the federal government funded new construction and supported artists under the rubric of the Works Projects Administration (WPA). Included was a new federal courthouse and post office in Aiken, South Carolina, a town that had garnered national attention in the 1920s when a mob killed black teenagers after their convictions had been overturned by the South Carolina Supreme Court.[35] The art commission went to Stefan Hirsch, who lived in the Northeast where he was a successful artist.[36]

Hirsch's mural *Justice as Protector and Avenger*,[37] measuring more than twelve-by-twelve feet, was installed in 1938 behind the judge's bench in a courtroom. At its center is a woman, Jus-

35. A fuller description can be found in Resnik and Curtis, *Representing Justice*, 110–13. Both this image and one of the "Indian" shown about to be lunched are reproduced, see color plates 19 and 21. See also Karal Ann Marling, *Wall-to-Wall America: A Cultural History of Post Office Murals in the Great Depression* (Minneapolis: University of Minnesota Press, 1982) 29; Marlene Park and Gerland E. Markowitz, *Democratic Vistas: Post Offices and Public Art in the New Deal* (Philadelphia: Temple University Press, 1984) 61; Sue Bridwell Beckham, *Depression Post Office Murals and Southern Culture: A Gentle Reconstruction* (Baton Rouge: Louisiana State University Press, 1989) 15, 44–45.

36. Hirsch, who died in 1964, taught at Bennington and at Bard Colleges. The quotes here come from materials published in Marling, Park and Markowitz, Bechman, or from Stefan Hirsch and Elsa Rogo Papers, 1926–1985 (Boxes 1–3 and 11) in the Archives of American Art, Smithsonian Institution, http://siris-archives.si.edu/ipac20/ipac.jsp?&profile=all&source=~!siarchives&uri=full=3100001~!216012~!0#focus or from the General Services Administration, Fine Arts Collection Archives and other materials. More detailed information and citations are at Resnik and Curtis, *Representing Justice*, 110–13 and 457–59.

37. My thanks to Susan Harrison, formerly of the Art-in-Architecture Program and to Kathryn Erickson and Erin Clay of the Collection of Fine Arts of the GSA for their generous help in obtaining historical materials. The Aiken building was subsequently named the Charles E. Simons Jr. Federal Courthouse after Judge Simons, who had served as the Chief Judge for the District of South Carolina from 1980 to 1986.

tice, referencing a Renaissance Virtue who has become familiar because she (often shown with scales, sword, billowing robes, and sometimes a blindfold) is used in courthouses around the world. Hirsch's Justice is an imposing figure, open eyed, wearing a blue skirt and bright red shirt, hair drawn back in a bun, barefoot, gesturing authoritatively. This style was reminiscent of the Mexican muralists with whom Hirsch had studied.

Interpretative materials written in the 1990s by staff at the General Services Administration (GSA), the agency now charged with overseeing federal buildings, described this Justice as raising a "nurturing right hand to those who live righteously," while her left hand "repels miscreants with a condemning gesture."[38] The scenes under the word "Protector" include rolling hills, cows, children playing, and a woman holding a baby. In contrast, under the label "Avenger," Hirsch portrayed crimes—a house burns, a man holds open a door to a prison cell through which a man (garbed in prison stripes) either enters or leaves while another man is crouching where a woman's body lies, with a shotgun below.

Hirsch explained that he created "a symbolic figure of 'Justice' with gestures indicating the meting out of justice to the deserving and the undeserving" and that his "gigantic female figure" was "without any of the customary or traditional appurtenances of such symbolic representations (scale, sword, book . . .) apparently stepping forth from an area of light into a dimmer world."[39]

38. The quoted text comes from the GSA exhibit brochure, "Images of Justice," a traveling exhibit drawing on several images from the Fine Arts program that were on tour in 2007–2008 in various courthouses in the United States. See http://www.gsa.gov/graphics/pbs/Justice_as_Protector.pdf.

39. See Archives of the General Services Administration and in the Hirsch papers at the Smithsonian at note 34 above. See also Parks and Markowitz, *Democratic Vistas*, 61; Marling, *Wall-to-Wall America*, 66.

Further, Justice was a "healthy, young person striding out forward with a determined step, clad in a simple garment which is neither modish nor classical, which displays the sturdy shape and balance without flaunting it, she carries her head proudly and in her glance shows no partiality. . . . [T]he only allegory I permitted myself was to use the red, white and blue [of the United States flag] for her garments."

That was not how others saw it. After the mural was installed, a local newspaper objected to the "barefooted mulatto woman wearing bright-hued clothing," while the sitting federal judge termed it a "monstrosity"—a "profanation of the otherwise perfection" of the courthouse. Hirsch argued that his Justice was an abstraction, "far from any ideas of caricature or racial issues." Within the month, the judge had "ordered that the mural be hidden with a cloth until it could be removed."

As the GSA subsequently described the events, federal officials attributed the criticisms to "ignorance" but offered a "compromise"— that the artist would "lighten Justice's skin color and cover the mural while court was in session." Archival materials reflect that Hirsch had written to government administrators that they could not find "ten reputable citizens of Aiken, not under the influence of the judge" who would "feel that the figure's face really appears to have negroid traits. I should not only be willing but anxious to obliterate this 'blemish,' because I had certainly intended nothing of the sort."

A government official responded: "I must confess that the palette of the head of the figure of Justice, the dark shadow and the vivid red lips, made me see the criticism of the local individuals involved as it would be easy to come to the conclusion that the figure is mulatto. This is especially true if one approached the work with suspicion to begin with. In the interests of your mural and its ultimate acceptance by Aiken I am asking you . . . [to] see if you cannot change the flesh tones of the main figure so that no one could possibly interpret the figure as a thrust at the South." Reminding Hirsch that a "federal judge has complete authority in his court room," he told Hirsch that, as an interim measure, he had recommended a "good velvet curtain on a pole with drawstrings" so the image could be covered when the judge wanted and otherwise "readily available" to be seen.

The mural was not, however, repainted. Apparently the judge urged the artist not to return, as "it would be impossible to touch that painting without running into more uncalled for publicity." The "controversy" was indeed attracting attention from various quarters, including the Artists' Union of Baltimore, which had asserted the sovereignty of the people ("The mural . . . was approved by . . . well-qualified and experienced judges of art. . . . It is now public property, paid for by citizens' taxes.") and demanded that the judge uncover the mural ("by arbitrarily ordering the painting covered and removed from the spectators' view, you have forced you[r] private opinion upon the public, denied citizens access to their common property, and grossly misused the power of your office"). The NAACP's Walter White argued that if the judge's "sole objection to the mural is the fact that the central figure is that of a person who is not white, then a new low in judicial conduct and racial prejudice would seem to have been reached." The judge countered that he was concerned that the imagery would be disruptive, particularly when sentencing criminals. Although the judge, aided by South Carolina's then governor, sought removal, the denouement was the installation of a tan velvet curtain covering the imagery.

This 1930s conflict about depiction is one of several making plain that certain figures could not pass, uncontested, into the deserving ranks of those who qualified to represent Justice.[40] Nor, in that era, could people labeled "mulattos" gain much protection from the courts as a matter of law. But fifty years later, long after the Supreme Court had decided *Brown v. Board of Education*, members of the Aiken community raised money to make the mural visible by relocating it to the Aiken County Judicial Center. Senator Strom Thurmond (who represented South Carolina in Congress from 1954 to 2003 and was once famous for his racist views) wrote in support of the move.

Conservators, however, deemed the mural too fragile to relocate, and it remained behind curtains. According to a local newspaper reporter writing in 2001, the mural was not displayed during court sessions because the "flamboyant green background and the vibrant clothes on Lady Justice" made the "power of the gavel pale." Instead, the curtains are parted and the mural shown only "by request."

Yet, in the same era that the "mulatto" Justice was covered as unsightly, another series of WPA murals were placed on the walls of the Ada County Courthouse in Idaho. One panel depicted "an Indian being lynched."[41] As a recent press report explained, the mural showed an "Indian in buckskin breeches, on his knees with his hands bound behind his back . . . flanked by a man holding a rifle and another armed man holding the end of a noose dangling from a tree."[42]

40. See Resnik and Curtis, *Representing Justice*, 108–25, for further examples and analyses.

41. Matthew Boedy, "Controversy Shadows Mural," *Augusta Chronicle*, August 26, 2001, C2.

42. John Miller, "Criticized Murals Hang in Courthouse," *Casper-Star Tribune*, May 15, 2005. The design likely came from Ivan Bartlett, building on sketches from Fletcher Martin; the murals were painted by various individuals. See Diana Cammarota, "Courthouse Murals," *Boise City Review* (2011), http:boisecityreview.com/posts/courthouse-murals.

No objections were recorded at the time to this display of what now could be described as a "low-tech" lynching. (A few did not like the painting itself.[43]) But towards the end of the late twentieth century, a judge (who later served as the chief justice of the Idaho Supreme Court) concluded that the imagery "would be offensive, and rightfully offensive, to some people."[44] The court ordered the mural draped with flags of the state and of the United States.

In 2006, when the Idaho state legislature was using the Ada County Courthouse as its temporary residence, the question debated was whether the mural ought to be painted over, preserved as it was, or displayed with new educational explanations of past prejudices. In 2007, the state legislative committee, reportedly guided by the views of local Indian tribes, decided that the murals were to remain on view, framed by "official interpretive signs"[45] because they reflected the values at that time.

Hill-Thomas likewise reflected the values of the time. In 1991, and now again twenty years later, the exchanges pull back the curtains and reveal several dimensions of the complex relationships among knowledge, authority, identity, and judgment. The 1991 reopening of the Thomas confirmation hearings serves as a reminder that collective action is required to have the power to insist on public proceedings. The interactions force onlookers to witness how women and men of color are treated, understood, heard, misheard, and depicted. Observers can begin to appreciate the roles played by gender and race in constituting authority and legitimacy. The brevity of the time accorded for reconsideration and the limited inquiry reveal the unwillingness

43. See "Idaho Artist Believes Apathy Toward New Murals Justified," *Idaho Statesman*, July 4, 1940, 10.

44. See Miller, "Criticized Murals."

45. John Miller, "Indian Leaders View Murals of Lynching," *Casper-Star Tribune*, January 19, 2007.

to unearth painful layers of interpersonal practices crisscrossing gender, race, and class. The anxiety of identity-based groups to be outspoken captures the awkward positions in which they sit—seeking to speak on behalf of constituencies (that likewise may be torn or conflicted) and aiming for authority and legitimacy. The ultimate vote—fifty-two votes for confirmation instead of the expected fifty-eight[46]—was both a victory and a loss, sealed by the short window of time and the aborted investigation.

Thus, the return to the events that produced Hill-Thomas both reveals injustices long tolerated as part of life's fabric and suggests how to weave new understandings of what justice—as a Virtue, a practice, and an aspiration—can look like.

JUDITH RESNIK is the Arthur Liman Professor of Law at Yale Law School, where she teaches about federalism, procedure, courts, equality, and citizenship. She also holds an appointment as an honorary professor in the Faculty of Laws at University College London. Resnik's books include *Representing Justice: Invention, Controversy, and Rights in City-States and Democratic Courtrooms* (with Dennis Curtis, 2011); *Migrations and Mobilities: Citizenship, Borders, and Gender* (co-edited with Seyla Benhabib, 2009); and *Federal Courts Stories* (co-edited with Vicki C. Jackson, 2010). Resnik is also an occasional litigator; she argued *Mohawk Industries, Inc. v. Carpenter*, decided in 2009 by the United States Supreme Court. Resnik has also testified before Congress, before rule-making committees of the federal judiciary, and before the House of Commons of Canada.

46. Three Democrats, Joseph Lieberman of Connecticut, Richard Bryan of Nevada, and Harry Reid of Nevada, who had been supportive of Thomas, changed their votes. Three other Democrats, Bob Graham of Florida, Daniel Moynihan of New York, and Robert Byrd of West Virginia, who had "hinted" support of Thomas, also voted against him. One cannot know whether, had more time been available, sufficient political will would have been marshaled through organizations shifting positions to have defeated the nomination.

VOICE, HEART, GROUND

CATHARINE A. MACKINNON

Word of what became the so-called big story of the face-off between Anita Hill and Clarence Thomas—big because the media decided to make it big, not because the facts of the harassment were so extreme or unusual; big because of the prominence of the man involved, no doubt; and in part, I think, because of big media's feel for the big white supremacist voyeurism around Black sexuality—first reached me in a public hot tub overlooking the Pacific. It was my birthday and everyone around me was suddenly talking about sexual harassment. What a present for someone who had pioneered the legal claim for sexual harassment as sex discrimination as a law student 20 years before,[1] back when, as Gloria Steinem has put it, sexual harassment was "just life."[2]

I spent the Hill-Thomas hearings inside NBC watching them virtually in their entirety on live feed, talking with Tom Bro-

1. The work begun as a law student paper was published as *Sexual Harassment of Working Women* (New Haven: Yale University Press, 1979).

2. This observation is reiterated in the documentary, *Gloria: In Her Own Words* (HBO 2011).

kaw on and off the air, preparing and presenting commentary.[3] It felt like being in touch with the entire country in a massive consciousness-changing session on a subject that I had been trying to make real to people other than those who did it or those who had it done to them for almost two decades.

By the way, this was back before the ideological maneuver had been completed making the term "victim" into a dirty word—a victim-blaming shift that casts the experience into a mold so falsely passive that no victimized person could, or would ever want to, recognize herself in it. That move came soon after in the fight against pornography, of which these hearings were also an important part.

What happened in the Hill-Thomas hearings, among other things, was that sexual harassment became real to the world at large for the first time. My book of 1979, framing the legal claim in the way that it became legally accepted,[4] did not do this. The EEOC Guidelines of 1980[5] did not do this. Winning Mechelle Vinson's case in the Supreme Court in 1986[6] did not do this, although all these helped prepare the way. Anita Hill did this: her still, fully present, utterly lucid testimony, that ugly microphone stuck in her beautiful face,[7] the unblinking camera gawking at her from point blank range.

3. These segments are available for viewing through the Vanderbilt Television News Archive, http://tvnews.vanderbilt.edu/.

4. MacKinnon, *Sexual Harassment of Working Women*.

5. Guidelines on Discrimination Because of Sex, 29 C.F.R. § 1604.11 (1980). http://www.eeoc.gov/policy/docs/harassment.html.

6. Meritor Savings Bank v. Vinson, 477 U.S. 57 (1986). I was co-counsel with Patricia Barry.

7. Anita Hill's testimony was broadcast live on C-SPAN, where it is archived in two installments. See http://www.c-spanvideo.org/program/22097-1; http://www.c-spanvideo.org/program/Day1Part3.

After she spoke out, complaints of sexual harassment tripled and quadrupled and more across the nation, in numbers where they have roughly stabilized.[8] Outrage over how she was treated by the Senate, political scientists documented, inspired a record number of women voters to support women candidates for public office and arguably elected Bill Clinton president.[9] Women everywhere realized that this isn't just life. It violates their civil and human rights. They mobilized, so now there are laws against sexual harassment all over the world.[10]

This happened because women identified with Professor Hill—with her dignity and her quality of presence. They believed her fiercely, and more said so as time and heat passed. Proudly, they saw her stand in the fire and come through it. They realized that what had been done to them was at least as unequal and violative as what had been done to her. When asked, she stood up to it. They wanted to be with her, came to feel that if she did this,

8. Statistics prior to 1992 are available in the U.S. Equal Employment Opportunity Commission [hereinafter "EEOC"] *Annual Reports* and *Combined Annual Reports*: (1981): 141; (1982): 54; (1983): 58; (1984): 20; (1985): 12; (1986): 18; (1987): 19; (1988): 20; (1990): 17; (1991): 28. Data for subsequent years can be found at Sexual Harassment Charges, EEOC & FEPAs Combined: FY 1992 - FY 1996, http://www. eeoc.gov/eeoc/statistics/enforcement/sexual_harassment-a.cfm; and EEOC, Sexual Harassment Charges, EEOC & FEPAs Combined: FY 1997 - FY 2011, http://www. eeoc.gov/eeoc/statistics/enforcement/sexual_harassment.cfm.

9. On the effect on electing women, see Susan J. Carroll, "The Politics of Difference: Women Public Officials as Agents of Change," *Stanford Law & Policy Review* 5 (1994): 11-20. For further discussion, see Michael X. Delli Carpini and Ester R. Fuchs, "The Year of the Woman? Candidates, Voters, and the 1992 Elections," *Political Science Quarterly* 108 (1993): 34-35. For some of the data from which one can deduce an impact on Clinton's election in 1992, see Virginia Sapiro with Pamela Johnson Conover, "The Variable Gender Basis of Electoral Politics: Gender and Context in the 1992 US Election," *British Journal of Political Science* 27 (1997): 507-508.

10. As of this writing, sexual harassment is variously illegal in 117 countries. UN Women, *Progress of the World's Women 2011-2012: In Pursuit of Justice* (New York: United Nations, 2011), 24, http://progress.unwomen.org/pdfs/EN-Report-Progress. pdf.

they could do this, in an almost a spiritual transference of finding voice, gaining heart, standing ground.

This was remarkable especially because the hearings were not in court and Clarence Thomas was put on the Supreme Court anyway. What women saw was not that she won, but that she counted. That seriousness has had her face ever since: an African-American woman's face. These are women who have long known that they had rights, before any lawyer or any court knew it.

So sexual harassment became both an outrage that mattered and a part of politics as usual for the first time, a real if complicated step up for women. No longer can powerful men—and men are socially powerful—be sure that the sexual abuse they inflict will be covered up. Few things have been the same since.

CATHARINE A. MACKINNON, Elizabeth A. Long Professor of Law at the University of Michigan Law School and James Barr Ames Visiting Professor of Law at Harvard Law School (long-term), specializes in sex equality issues under international, constitutional, and criminal law. She pioneered the legal claim for sexual harassment and, with Andrea Dworkin, created ordinances recognizing pornography as a civil rights violation and the Swedish model for abolishing prostitution. Her books include *Sex Equality* (2001/2007), *Toward a Feminist Theory of the State* (1989), *Only Words* (1993), *Women's Lives, Men's Laws* (2005), and *Are Women Human?* (2006). Representing Bosnian women and children survivors of Serbian genocidal sexual atrocities, she won with co-counsel a damage award of $745 million in August 2000 in *Kadic v. Karadzic*, which first recognized rape as an act of genocide. MacKinnon received a BA from Smith College, a JD from Yale Law School, and a PhD in political science from Yale. She served as the Special Gender Adviser to the Prosecutor of the International Criminal Court (The Hague) implementing her concept "gender crime" from 2008 to 2012.

BUT I COULD BE

JAMIA WILSON

Professor Anita Hill's endurance and resilience has inspired my generation to stand up for ourselves, live authentically, and trust in our outrage in the face of grave injustice.

I'm here to speak about witnessing the hearings through the media as a tween and to share how they ignited my click moment of feminist realization and the development of my personal identity as a young black feminist.

Prior to Anita Hill, my definition of women's rights extended mostly to what impacted me personally. I believed that I was just as smart as any boy and was annoyed that boys were called on more often in class than girls. I didn't like having to stand outside of the men-only record store in Saudi Arabia where I grew up, while my dad entered alone to buy me censored Janet Jackson CDs. I had to rely on my dad or taxis to drive me everywhere, because women were not and still are not permitted to drive in the kingdom.

I remember knowing that I was a Democrat, because I accompanied my family to progressive campaign events. I recall attending a civil rights march to challenge the wrongful firing of an African American teacher in North Carolina. However, I had no real connection to feminist activism or organizing until the Hill-Thomas hearings.

When I was contemplating this anniversary, I reflected on my friend Jamil Smith's tweet and Facebook message in the aftermath of Troy Davis's state-mandated murder. Jamil tweeted: I AM NOT TROY DAVIS, but I could be. Later Jamil and I spoke about it and he said that if he made a T-shirt, it would say: "I AM NOT TROY DAVIS. But I could be. And it scares the crap out of me." Reflecting on his wisdom, I immediately thought, I AM NOT ANITA HILL. But I could be. And that scares the crap out of me.

And this is why witnessing the hearings as an eleven-year-old child impacted me and transformed my view of the world and my place in it.

It was a year after the Gulf War, which had rattled my community, causing me and my family to briefly leave our quiet expat existence and return to the US. Nineteen ninety-one was the year I watched *Thelma and Louise* with my parents on a bootlegged tape that was passed around our compound in Riyadh. That film and the Hill-Thomas hearings introduced me to the grim reality of a victim-blaming, rape-shaming culture. When I think back to what I witnessed and experienced during the Anita Hill trial, I remember a lengthy road trip with my parents to visit family and friends in Georgia and South Carolina. We were back in the US visiting after an eventful year in Saudi Arabia where we had lived for about five years. I recall riding in my father's new jeep, listening to the start of the hearings on the radio for the entire ride. At the time, I wasn't aware of how historically important Anita Hill's testimony would be to my life and the lives of women across the nation. But I was aware that it must be critical for my dad to opt to hear the testimony over his usual soundtrack of Motown, old soul, and gospel during our trips.

I remember my parents focusing on every word, being drawn in by the banter, and cheering at the testimony of progressives. As liberal professors, my parents were the kind of so-called "uppity blacks" Clarence Thomas was claiming to be in solidarity with in his desperate quest to fuel fear and garner sympathy.

I also recollect sitting in the back seat pretending to read *The Baby-Sitters Club* while leaning in, listening, and wondering what Long Dong Silver was, and thinking that I might never drink a Coca-Cola again.

After listening to the first day of the hearings on the radio, we spent the next few days watching it in hotel rooms and in the homes of friends. I recall thinking about a play I had seen, *The Crucible*, and contemplating the dreadful way former Senator Alan Simpson and Orrin Hatch interrogated Hill, resenting her credibility, decency, intelligence, and, most of all, it seemed, her race and gender. As Hill was accused of perjury and Simpson warned us to "watch out for this woman," I became aware that we were living a modern day witch hunt rather than a so-called high-tech lynching described by Thomas.

My mom has always said that I was born thirty-five years old. I guess she was right. I always fought to make sure I sat at the adult table because all of the juicy conversations happened there. At dinner, a family friend brought up the hearings and constructed Thomas as a martyr in need of being saved by all "conscious blacks." This friend felt the need to protect Thomas's honor with the same vigor as he would his own. He saw Thomas as a black man who was paving the way for others to "arrive" and achieve the same sort of upward mobility in spite of his conservative outlook.

I cringed when my father said that he thought Anita Hill was lying and that she was just angry because Clarence Thomas dated white women. He presented the possibility of a conspiracy theory between Hill and the white establishment, designed to block Thomas from his rightful place in the court, in an act of resentment toward all black masculinity.

At that moment, I wasn't thinking about how to unpack all of the baggage connected to his assertion, but I knew it created a knot in my stomach, and made me feel as if someday I too could be marked a traitor if I somehow stepped out of line by challenging patriarchy within my community and beyond. I understood then that for some, being black was about normalizing and celebrating black masculinity at all costs, even if this erased or undervalued the realities of black women.

Without knowing it, I was getting an introductory education about intersectionality. Responding to my father's claims, I retorted, "Well, I believe Anita Hill. I am a feminist." I remember it as clear as day because my father laughed, took a swig of Crown Royal and looked around the dinner table at the other adults. He gave me one of those "isn't she cute" pats on my head and said, "Lawd, she said she's a feminist. Girl, you are not a feminist. You could maybe be a womanist if you are anything at all, and you don't even know what that means." I had not yet been acquainted with the theories of Alice Walker, Kimberlé Crenshaw, and Patricia Hill Collins, but I knew that it was wrong for him to tell me who I could and couldn't be and how to define myself. I decided then that I was a feminist—and eventually a womanist too once I found out what it meant.

Anita Hill made it possible for me and many others to feel empowered to speak up. She fought to reveal the truth without fear, in spite of being portrayed as an attention-seeking race traitor by some, and jezebel stereotype by others. The character assassination she experienced and the disparaging words I heard spoken by friends, schoolmates, and family deepened my faith in the truth of her testimony.

Recently, I was moved when I saw the Occupy Wall Street video about an approach to building a movement and creating a new world together through consensus. Even though Occupy Wall Street isn't perfect, and has its own work to do to transcend the clutches of hierarchy and oppression, I imagined what Hill's testimony would have been like in a true democracy—in a society free of patriarchy, heterosexism, ableism, racism, and white supremacy. Clarence Thomas would have never been confirmed, and the justice that would be appointed and confirmed to the highest court in our land would be more like you, like me, or Professor Anita Hill.

While it is often demoralizing that we still have a long way to go, I remain hopeful. I'll continue to work diligently to amplify women's voices and hold media accountable for victim blaming and shaming, and *change* the conversation in the media with the Women's Media Center because I AM NOT ANITA HILL—but I could be.

JAMIA WILSON is a feminist activist, organizer, ex-pat-brat, networker, cartwheeler, truth-seeker, and storyteller. She is currently vice president of programs at the Women's Media Center (WMC). She trains women and girls so they are media ready and media savvy, exposes sexism in the media, and directs the WMC's social media strategy. Before joining WMC, she worked for Young People for the American Way, the Planned Parenthood Action Fund, and Planned Parenthood Federation of America where she managed their youth outreach program. After working with coalition partners and campus organizations to help bring thousands of students to the historic March for Women's Lives, Wilson was honored as one of the Real Hot 100 by the Younger Women's Taskforce.

DON'T GET ME STARTED ON
THESE WOMEN . . .

LISA KRON

I supported myself for the first ten years I lived in New York as an office temp, working mostly in law offices. It was kind of a wildly split existence—with my days spent in these midtown offices, and every night and weekend spent working in a lesbian theater collective in the East Village. In the office setting, I was clearly a misfit—neither professional nor appropriate in the way I dressed and I was always being spoken to about it. I think I believed I was being rebellious, but in retrospect I was just contrary—I was always trying to get other women outraged about the things I found outrageous in office hierarchy. For instance, it was extremely common then for a secretary's salary base to be based on the status of the lawyer she worked for. So the secretary of a partner would make more than the secretary of an associate, regardless of her age or level of experience. I found this appalling and was always trying to organize the secretaries around this issue and they were always looking at me like, Who are you? What are you talking about? They thought I was strange and I thought they were strange. Between me and these women, there were a million tiny cultural disconnects and also a kind of mutual fascination.

This is where I was when the Thomas-Hill hearings happened, moving between my very politicized nights and weekends with the lesbians into these days filled with women who had a kind of reflexive skepticism about Anita Hill and her story. And I wondered what was at stake for these women in not believing Anita Hill's story. What did things look like from the other side of this cultural divide? And trying to imagine the world from this view, I wrote this monologue for a secretary, whom I pictured to be an "older" secretary; in other words, about the age I am now. I pictured her speaking in a Long Island accent; I had only recently come to New York from the Midwest, and the manner and language of these Long Island and New Jersey ladies was completely exotic and delicious to me. I pictured her sitting in a midtown salad bar lunch place; another secretary has just asked if she can sit in the empty seat next to her:

What? Oh yeah. Of course. Sit sit sit sit sit.

This? Tortellini. It's nice. Yeah, it's a nice salad bar. I don't usually come out for lunch.

Have I been what? Oh, my God, the hearings! Of course I'm watching. You can't get away from it! Listen, you're not going to get any argument from me on that. I agree. It's a mess. The whole thing is a mess!

What? Yeah, I work around the corner at Bochner, Stiffner, and Krinsky. I work for Mr. Krinsky. He's a partner. Yeah, he's a partner. Of course, I get compensated accordingly. Some of the ones now, they don't agree with that. One of the temps—I don't know her name—I make it my business never to learn the names of temps, I call them all Cathy, if I need to talk to one I say, "Hey, you, Cathy," and when she tells me her name, I say,

"Oh, I don't know, the last girl's name was Cathy"—these temps come in off the street and they act like they own the place. You're out a day with the flu and when you come back everything on your desk is in a different place. Why? Why is that? Why do they have to touch everything? My three-hole punch! I use my three-hole maybe three times a year, a temp is there for one day, it's in a completely different place and all jammed up with the paper—where was I?

—Oh right, so one day I walk into the lunchroom and this temp is holding forth, lord knows how she got started, but she's holding forth about how all secretaries should be paid the same or some other bullcrap and I thought I was going to blow my top. I mean, if she knows so much about how things are sup- posed to work, how come she can't get a job of her own and she has to travel from office to office dressed like a . . . like a . . . circus-hobo. These people come in from the outside think- ing they know all about you and how you are supposed to want things to be, but I'll tell you, Mr. Krinsky is not easy. He is not easy and he is lucky to have me and I deserve to be paid accord- ingly and that's that, that's all I have to say about that, where were we . . . ? Oh right, the hearings. Listen, I have never worked for a woman, but I have seen these woman attorneys for years. My best girlfriend Eileen, from the old firm, she worked for this woman for a while—the stories Eileen told me, and, of course, I saw it. I saw how she was. She was driven. That woman worked like a dog and she worked Eileen like a horse and a dog. She was high powered, that one, with the Chanel suits and the this and the that. She was—you know what she was like? She was like that Rosalind Chaise on the *LA Law*. And the personal things! She wanted Eileen to pick up her dry cleaning. Now, you know, the men give you that stuff a lot. Mr. Krinsky? I balance his daughter's checkbook, for God's sake. Look, I don't mind. If I did, I would tell him. But the point is, the men don't know any better. But the women? They should know. Eileen did it. She did it. But when another spot opened up she told the administrator that she wanted it or she was leaving and they moved her, they didn't want to lose her. But they went through a lot of temps before they got someone else to work for that woman because people looked at her and they knew. They knew what she was like, and they did not want to deal with that.

You saw that senator, right? Who was saying about all those people who wrote to him, people who had worked for that . . . Anita. Wrote to him saying "Do not believe the act." You see? This is exactly the kind of person, this is the kind of person I'm talking about. She didn't want to lose her job, she was so dedicated to her career. Let me tell you something, these women lawyers can work over a secretary until she is so much as dust on the carpet and you're going to tell me that one couldn't tell this man where to go with his can of coke and his pubic hair? I don't think so.

Oh my God. People in our office are worked up into a lather over this mess. It's like a pressure cooker atmosphere. And, this on top of we're having one of those virus things on the computer—have you had this? Every time you put a disk into the machine all of a sudden with the beeping and the flashing. Mary Anne who sits next to me, this morning her machine went off. She nearly had a heart attack, literally, a heart attack! I got up, I walked all the way around the partition. I said Mary Anne, press the P to proceed. P. P. P. P to proceed. Do something, hit something, for God's sake put yourself out of your misery. And she's there with her hands up like paws or something and I said, Mary Anne what is wrong with you? And she says to me: I don't want to catch the virus from the computer. And I said, Tell Mr. Krinsky I'm going to lunch, I'd told him I was going to work through but by that time I'd had it. I went downstairs to the cafeteria—yeah, we have a cafeteria for the employees. It's nice, a little expensive, it's nice. I got a nice stir fry. And I sat. And I said, Mr. Krinsky is not going to die if he has to answer the phone for fifteen minutes while I eat a lunch in peace. And I was doing the breathing—have you done this? I saw it on Channel Thirteen, the deep breathing, the visualization, the colors, the waves, the beach thing. I don't go overboard with it. For some people, it's like a cult or something, I don't go overboard, I like to keep an open mind, whatever. So here I am with my lunch and my blue bubble of serenity and the conversation next to me is getting louder and louder with these women going on and on and on about the hearings, and I think, my God, can I not have one minute to eat a lunch in peace? I threw the whole plate in the garbage, I went to Duane Reade, I bought a moisturizer, I came here and got the . . . the tortellini.

Yeah, I'll tell you what I think. It's disgusting. Seeing these people's dirty laundry aired out in public like that. Those senators are disgusting—all of them, Democrat, Republican, I don't care, they're disgusting pigs. At least that Ted Kennedy knows what a disgusting pig he is. You can see he is not looking forward to the miniseries on him. Listen, I shouldn't judge. One brother shot, another brother shot. Probably, maybe, he thought, I'm next, I might as well have some fun, I don't know, and then with the son, with the leg, God bless him, God bless him my point is: you can tell he knows those hearings don't belong on TV. What happened was private, between two people.

Why is she doing this? This is what I can't understand. Maybe, I don't know, I think maybe she *was* in love with him. Why is she doing this??? She has a good career, teaching at that school. And I'll tell you, I get sick of the whining these girls do now about the this and the that and they want everything handed to them and they're spoiled, these girls, and then complaining and complaining and complaining because, because. . . I don't know why. I think they want to feel special. I think they like the attention. I don't know. I don't know. Apparently they don't realize that life is not easy for anybody. Things happen. When you're young, things happen and you don't know how to . . . You can't . . . When you're young you don't know how to say, "Zip that up. Put that away . . . Don't, don't . . . touch me like that." Look, things . . . happen . . . to people. And they feel . . . Yes, you feel bad at the time, but you can't take away what's done and you can't make a mess in the place where you live, and so you move on. You move on. That girl, that temp, in an office for few days, for a week, I think it does not occur to her that you cannot make a big mess in the place where you have to live. Oh my God, don't get me started. Do not get me started on the temps. My God, look at the time! I've gotta get back before Mr. Krinsky has a conniption fit. It was nice talking to you. By the way, I like that jacket on you, it's a very flattering style. All right then, okay, you too, okay, bye bye.

LISA KRON has been writing and performing theater since coming to New York from Michigan in 1984. In 2006, her play *Well* opened to critical acclaim on Broadway and received two Tony nominations. Her play *2.5 Minute Ride* premiered at La Jolla Playhouse in 1996 and then in New York at the Public Theater in 1999, and received an OBIE Award, Drama Desk and Outer Critics Circle nominations. Kron is a founding member of the OBIE and Bessie Award-winning theater company The Five Lesbian Brothers, whose plays, *Oedipus at Palm Springs*, *Brave Smiles*, *Brides of the Moon* and *The Secretaries* have all been produced by their theatrical home, New York Theater Workshop, and have been performed widely throughout the country both by the Brothers and by other companies. She teaches playwriting at Yale Drama School.

PART II

RESPONDERS: WHAT DOES ANITA HILL
MEAN TO YOU?

NITA FAYE

ASALI DEVAN ECCLESIASTES

Sometimes I can't stand my mama friends. They call too early on Saturday mornings and too late on Sunday nights. They always tryna get somebody in trouble wit' what they seen. Always tryna tell my mama how to raise us, cause they kids is older, like that mean sumthin'. And always talkin' bout somebody, half the time somebody they don't even know! Especially Mrs. Janice, who pronounces her name "Juh-niece" and always startin' her sentences with "Girl yeah." I hate that. She came home with my mama after work yesterday. I hate that too. I wanna tell Mama the same thing she be tellin' me when I talk to my friends on the phone. "You been with her all day. What y'all got to talk about?"

So they come sit at the kitchen table where I'm doin' my homework and ask me to get up to make them some plates of leftover gravysteaks. "I'm doin' my homework," I say, tryin' not to roll my neck.

My mama say, "Don't forget the spinach 'n' potatoes. Boil an egg for my spinach and gimme two horses first . . . wit'out poppin' ya neck Ms. Thang. Next time Imma have to smack you."

I didn't even have the luxury of grumbling under my breath with them sitting right there, so I stuck my face into the icebox and took a long time looking for the Miller High Lifes.

I was glad when Mrs. Janice started up. It took my mother's attention off of me. "Girl yeah," she began, "you know Nita Faye is a midwest farm girl, can't take no joke."

My mama say, "Who?"

Mrs. Janice laughs, "Girl you know, Nita Faye, up there in front the congressmen, actin' all sadiddy, like she all that, but now, she know what it is." I think, I know she not talkin' bout Anita Hill!

My mama say, "I know you not talkin' bout Anita Hill."

She say, "Girl yeah, I'm sho tireda all this nonsense with her. I'm glad they voted and gon' go ahead and give that Brotha his due."

My mama say, "He's due a kick in the ass."

She say, "Huh! At the most. What he ain't due is to have all his accomplishments go down the drain cause of this foolishness."

I locate the beers behind the milk and notice they're only two left, and one is a smaller bottle. Uncle Poochie must've been over while we were at school. I place the larger bottle in front of my mother and say, "One horse," then in an effort to get sent to my room, slam the other in front of Mrs. Janice and say, "One pony!"

Mama pinched me hard on the thigh and said, "Quit talking like you work in a barroom!"

Mrs. Janice laughed, switched the beers and said, "Careful, you gon' getchu a hearing like Clarence, you keep pinching that girl's ass." Why she always talkin' bout people like she know them! Rubbing the sore spot on my thigh, I stomped back to the icebox to take out last night's leftovers.

"So seriously, Janice" my mama says, "you think they made the right decision. That it's okay for a man who treats his employees like that to be on the Supreme Court? What if Ray did that to you?" My mama and Mrs. Janice worked together at the phone company. My mama was the dispatch supervisor and Mrs. Janice was the general manager's secretary. She made a big deal about being called his "administrative assistant."

"Girl, Ray know better than to play with me like that—or his wife. We would slap the taste out his mouth," she followed with an amused laugh. "But don't think it ain't neva happen to me before. Shit, you know it happens to most all of us. At the university . . ."

I began to tune them out. I wasn't interested in Mrs. Janice's nine hundred and ninety ninth different rendition of how she kept the Early Childhood Education Department at Tulane with their checks early because the notoriously austere and behind schedule comptroller got weak whenever she walked into the room. Especially not the "girl!" and "chile!" filled dramatic ending, where she barely escapes a mauling in the parking lot, when he, as my grampa would say, acted on his ambitions. I think, I don't want it to happen to me and I don't wanna be used to it. I don't want men being able to make me uncomfortable because they're my boss, talkin' bout porn and dicks and pubic hairs. And on-time checks, for kisses on the cheek and smacks on the ass that make everybody think I'm a ho. And fighting off attacks, and can't get raises, and can't get respect. I'm not gon' be like my mama n'em. Cause I know they not like my gramma n'em. My gramma n'em usedta could get raped by their husbands, couldn't have their own money or rights to their own children. Let's not even think about Gramma n'em Gramma. She didn't even own her own self, didn't have a right to her thoughts or dreams or even her name.

I tune back in to hear Mama argue, "So you mean to tell me that if that man was being promoted to president of Tulane and they came asking you what it was like to work with him, that you wouldn't mention what he did because it's ten years later? Shit, if it wasn't for what he did, you probably wouldn't remember him at all."

Mrs. Janice said, "No lie, I would swallow my pride, 'cause it's about damn time there was a black president at Tulane University."

Mama said, "Humph, true we've swallowed for less." She and Mrs. Janice giggle. They think I don't get it. They're so square.

Mama continues, "But for him to call it a lynchin' is hilarious. When has anyone ever got lynched for disrespectin' a black woman?"

Mrs. Janice countered, "She complain' bout words! When has anyone ever said anything to a black woman that she couldn't handle with the cut of her eye or the roll of her neck?"

Mama came back with laughter, "You wasn't sayin' that when Mr. Kaufman was tryna slip his tongue between ya cleavage."

Mrs. Janice howled, "That wasn't words chile, that was spit. Plus if I was making the kinda money she was, girl, I woulda took one for the team. Now bitches gon be comin' out the woodwork tryna get paid for playin' footsie at work."

My mother dissolved into laughter, "Girl, hush! You too crazy, them children is here!" I smacked my teeth loud, thinking, it ain't us children you need to be worryin' bout!

Mama turned to me and said, "You must be lookin for that smack!"

I answer, "Food's ready!" and place the plates in front of them with a flourish. Mama ain't smacked me in seven years, since the last time I lied to her. Now, I just don't tell her stuff.

"Y'all are welcome," I sass as I gather up my papers with an even greater flourish and stomp off to my brothers' room to finish my homework. I can't do it in my room because I always fall asleep. I can't wait to go away to college next year, I think, and begin fantasizing about my life without my mama and her friends. Mrs. Janice was kinda crazy, but I did like the name she came up with for Ms. Anita Hill and I wondered if people close to her might actually call her that. It was a name that made me think I could ask her things. Things I wouldn't ask anyone but her, but I wouldn't dare ask even her, unless we were close enough for me to call her Nita Faye. I would ask her things about Clarence Thomas—like did his breath smell? He seems like his breath would smell, which would make everything all the worse. I would ask her, because I think she would tell me the truth, like she's been doing all along though it would be so much easier for her to lie.

My homework for civics class was to write a reaction to the outcome of the hearings. I was writing a poem for you called "Ms. Hill" when Mama and her sidekick got here and started treating me like their waitress, but I think I'm gonna change the name to Nita Faye and go around the corner, see what Ms. Julie thinks about it. I don't read my poems to Mama no more, since she told me I use to many "ents" and "shuns" in my rhymes and my style is inconsistent. What about the content, Mother? I hear her walking Mrs. Janice to the door. I shake my head and start speaking my poem out loud for the first time, see how it feels on my tongue:

How you feel Nita Faye?
Since they confirmed him anyway?
Found your truth inconvenient
his cover-up expedient

said they would be fair
but didn't mean it.
Good ol' Geechee boy
never meanin' no harm
just got Geechee boy charm
sat with other Geechee babies
in crab basket bassinets
where maybe they learned to
imitate the behavior of the creatures
whose prison they occupied
while his mother and the other
Geechee women jived
as they shucked, picked, and plucked
to meet their fifteen-pound-a-day quotas
for jobs that paid in pennies
and the benefits were costly
because after all pussy and dignity
when they're yours, are priceless.
What did he learn from shift managers?
I know crabs weren't
the only things pinching.
That women are the boss, right?
We come with the job, right?
That's why he didn't get it
when you told him
your ass wasn't up for grabs
and he thought he could get it
if he just picked up a few tabs.
He wondered, who did you think you are?
Were you better than his mother and the others?
Those good Geechee women who

even with their good men gone
handled the home with never a hint
that anything was wrong
managed what to cook for dinner
with pittance in the pantry
and invading hands in
their splits with equal cool
and here you go, Nita Faye,
letting yourself be a political tool
to bring a good black man down,
don't matter that he let you down,
why wasn't the way he treated you
more of a let down?
It was the wrong time for truth.
52—48, they decided our fate
in the latest round of woman v. man
the women lose.

Mama shouts from front door, "The women lose? Whatchu in there babbling bout, girl? Come on out the boys room and show me your homework, now that Janice is gone. She done wore me out . . . sometimes I can't stand my friends!"

ASALI DEVAN ECCLESIASTES is a mother, educator, event producer, and spoken word artist. She is the co-founder and executive producer of the Akoben Words-In-Action Festival, a four-day poetry and community service event in New Orleans. She teaches spoken word, social justice, and service learning at Tulane University. She is also the coordinator of the Congo Square African Marketplace at the New Orleans Jazz and Heritage Festival, the largest music and arts festival in the world.

WHAT DOES ANITA HILL MEAN TO YOU?

PAT MITCHELL
JOANNE N. SMITH
AI-JEN POO
EMILY MAY
MELISSA V. HARRIS-PERRY
RHA GODDESS

Pat Mitchell: Joanne, your work engages a generation of girls and boys who may not know the name Anita Hill or remember her testimony and the impact. What do you remember and how do you make it meaningful and relevant to today's young people?

Joanne N. Smith: At the time of the hearings, I was sixteen years old. And what was so meaningful to me was seeing a woman who was giving voice to our ancestors. I'm first generation Haitian, born in the United States, so Anita Hill's speaking out gave voice to the experience that our ancestors had, but couldn't speak about. It also provided a language and definition of sexual harassment in the workplace for many women, including my own mother, who at the time just saw sexual harassment at the workplace as part of the job. The hearings gave a context for being able to deconstruct the institutions which impede equality.

For young people today, especially the young people I work with at Girls for Gender Equity (GGE), there are still so many obstacles to equality. At GGE, we are working hard in the New York City Public Schools for uniform implementation of Title IX, as well as other local and state policies, in order to protect all students—boy, girl, transgender, lesbian, gay, bisexual—from sexual harassment and gender-based violence.

Title IX of the education amendment has been around since 1972, but it's not uniformly implemented. In simple terms, there's not even a Title IX coordinator identified for the one thousand, seven hundred schools in New York City, so if there is a grievance by a student around sexual harassment or gender-based violence, they don't know who to go to. So then they are silenced, as Anita was initially, and that's why they don't tell. And that's also why they don't go to school. They end up accepting that this is what's going to happen and that no one will do anything about it. Our work is to be sure that schools are held accountable, and that in addition to there being people assigned this responsibility, there is follow through and investigations into the grievances. We don't want there to be further policing of people of color in schools; we must be able to provide education as well as support for youth development and advocacy so that young people can understand that social norms which play out in schools are microcosms of society, and they have the power to change that.

At GGE, we start with young people when they are in elementary school and stay with them through middle and high school. We meet them where they are at right now; not as a future baby mama or as a future Joanne. We start by understanding what they are dealing with without assuming that we know because we have been there, but respecting that they are the experts of their experience, as well as realizing that intergenerational support might be missing, and should be mandatory.

We are fighting a war against women and girls, and we have to prepare our young people to be leaders in this fight. If our government were to send soldiers off to war without boot camp, training, or understanding, whether it's right or wrong to go to war, we wouldn't allow it. This is how our young people are growing up. At GGE, to our best ability, we prepare our young people through consciousness-raising activities, and building sisterhood so they can go off to college and face the complexities of the violence and pornography that they're inundated with online. They discuss these issues in ways that didn't start for me until I was in college. At sixteen, I didn't have the language for what was happening to me; the youth of today understand and think critically about what's happening and understand that they have a role in affecting change.

It wasn't until I was an adult that I realized the shoulders that we're standing on, and the responsibility we have to pass on that understanding. We have a living legend who sacrificed the trajectory of her career and her life, to give voice because it was really the right thing to do. We have the tools to do the same thing. We don't have to be scholars and academics to be able to do that. We just have to be willing.

I call the generation now, the "unintended consequence of the Anita hearings." We are the feminists, the womanists, who are angry and don't see sexual harassment and gender-based violence as the norm. This is something that we need to eradicate.

Pat Mitchell: Ai-jen, your work in organizing domestic workers has had great impact on important issues of discrimination, pay structures, work conditions for a large group of people whose issues have not had a public voice or a way to bring to the public attention the many issues that they are coping with today. Recently, with the Dominique Strauss Kahn case, in which a domestic worker brought charges of sexual attack, put this issue of violence and abuse in the workplace on the front pages. But the way it played out was discouraging to say the least. How do you assess the damage of this particular case on the overall case of domestic workers and their rights?

Ai-jen Poo: When Aissatou Ba (aka Dominique Strauss Kahn's accuser) spoke out, she spoke for so many immigrant women workers who are vulnerable in their workplaces and face a lot of fear as a result of immigration status and exclusion from any protections. There are so many women in workplaces around the country who, through a tremendous amount of courage, speak out. I think many women were encouraged by her honesty and felt spoken for, and yet when the case was dismissed it was a reminder of how much work we have yet to do and how important women's organizing and activism is, particularly working women's organizing and activism. At the end of the day, we have to continue to speak out and fight for change, take collective action so that these cases are not seen as isolated cases that can be dismissed, but that ultimately we have to work together to change and transform the environment.

Domestic workers are continuing that fight. There are millions of women who go to work everyday as nannies, housekeepers and caretakers for the elderly. They do the work that makes all other work possible. It's important and valuable. In this economic climate, it's even harder on women. Women are always the last to be hired and the first to be fired. And to this day in this country, they are excluded from almost every major labor protection, including the protection from discrimination and harassment in the workplace. New York is the only exception because domestic workers organized for six years and passed a Domestic Workers Bill of Rights that was signed into law in 2010 that provides protection from discrimination and harassment. We have a bill being proposed in California that does the same right now and more states are going to follow. This is just a reminder of how important women's organizing is and how important it is to continue to speak truth to power.

We take concepts like intersectionality as movement-building and organizational principles. The framework of intersectionality offers a way to think about and organize in situations of complexity. For example, take some of the anti-immigrant state laws that have been passed in the last year or so, starting with Arizona, and then Georgia and Alabama. The less commonly told story about the anti-immigrant legislation is that it's creating a climate where local police can enforce immigration policy and racial profiling is essentially sanctioned. This creates a climate of fear of the police, of any public office or services, such as hospitals and shelters. These anti-immigrant laws are essentially rolling back decades of work done by the women's movement to break the silence around violence against women, which makes this very much a violence against women issue and a human rights issue for women everywhere. I think intersectionality allows us to see that and allows us to organize from that place.

When the law passed in Arizona, we took a delegation of women's leaders from throughout the country, including Ellen Bravo who was at the helm of 9 to 5 [the National Association of Working Women] for decades, to Arizona. Within a week's time, this group agreed to spend Mother's Day in

Arizona, away from their own children, documenting the stories of women in Arizona, the human rights violations that they were facing as a result of these laws. Then they came back to DC, convened women's organizations nationally and organized three congressional briefings to call on women members of Congress to take action against these anti-immigrant laws. It shows you when you look at the world through an intersectional lens and look at the ways in which we can bridge issues, across sectors, across constituencies, there's tremendous power there. I want to make sure to appreciate the tools that the women's movement has brought to bear, particularly women of color, and how powerful they are in the face of a lot of complexity.

It's the power of women coming together that offers the support and the context to continue to speak out despite what you risk in terms of being blamed. That's why Domestic Workers United has general meetings every month where women come together and they share their stories and realize that they're not alone. Even if the media is blaming them, even if there is no one else who believes them, they are reminded that there will be other women who are going to stand with them. There are now thirty-five domestic worker organizations in nineteen cities in eleven states around the country and we are coming together all the time.

Pat Mitchell: Emily, where did you personally get the message that it's not your fault and that it's all right to stand up against harassment?

Emily May: We founded Hollaback in 2005. I was twenty-four-years-old. It was the power of the workplace harassment movement that gave us the confidence that we could actually do something about street harassment.

At the time, we were just a group of friends, three guys and four women, and we started telling our stories. We felt that if it happened in the workplace, we would have some sort of response, but what's the difference between harassment that happens on the street and what happens in the workplace, other than location? The fact that we didn't have that response on the street angered us. But it was our own privilege in growing up with a response to workplace harassment that gave us the platform and those shoulders to stand on as we talked about street harassment.

I grew up knowing that it wasn't okay, and if it did happen to me, and it did, that it wasn't my fault and there was something I could do about it. I want to give that privilege to the next generation of activists so that when harassment happens to them on the street they know that it's not okay.

The first time I actually heard the message that it wasn't my fault was when everyone was talking about Anita Hill and sexual harassment. Nobody was talking about it to me directly, which I thought had to do with the fact that sexual harassment had the word "sex" in it and I was only ten. I asked my mom and she explained that Clarence Thomas had done a lot of inappropriate things and asked her on dates. But I pushed her: "If my stepfather did that to you, wouldn't you think that that was a compliment?" And she said, "Yes, but that's the man I'm married too. This is a nonconsensual relationship." And it was the first time that clicked in my mind, that things happen that were nonconsensual and that women just had to put up with them.

It's important to remember that people have a right to dress as they wish. It's about their right to be who they are. Sexual harassment disproportionately happens to women and girls, but it also happens to LGBT individuals and people of color. One of our volunteers told me, "When I get harassed on the street, I don't know if it's because I'm a woman, or a person of color or because I'm queer." You can't put it all in these boxes. Recently, there was a serial rapist in Brooklyn, and by way of "protection" the NYPD started pulling women aside and telling them that their shorts were too short. Public outrage ensued, six thousand people signed a petition advocating for police sensitivity, and following a late night meeting we had with them, they stepped back and agreed that that would no longer be their policy.

Harassment takes many forms. For example, how many people have been told to smile on the street, which really means: perform your gender! There are complex reasons why we may be harassed. It's not hopeless. Ending street harassment is about stepping up, using our voices, and sharing our stories. Be an activist on this issue, write about this work, and exclaim at the top of our lungs that it's not okay. We have to use those exclamations to shift a culture that makes gender-based violence okay. Day-to-day discrimination is not okay.

The workplace harassment movement did a stellar job of moving this through the courts, but when we talk about the street harassment movement, laws are looked at very suspiciously, particularly by low-income people and people of color who know that those laws are going to be disproportionately used against them. "What am I going to do? Grab this guy by the wrist and drag him to the police station?" women ask us. It's not a realistic solution. We really have to use cultural change, as ambiguous and hard to measure as it is, to shift the conversation to the broader cultural force which make things like street harassment, workplace harassment, rape, sexual assault so common. It starts by using your voice and having a genuine understanding that it's okay to be you, no matter who you are.

We have built Hollaback on the power of people's stories. And it's built on acknowledging that when people come forward bravely and boldly to tell their stories, so often they're raked over the coals. With the power of anonymity and the Internet we have been able to let people anonymously tell their stories. Thousands of people, in fifty cities and sixteen countries and nine different languages tell their stories. Through that compilation, and the solidarity it creates, we can stand up and define what street harassment means for all of us in this generation.

Pat Mitchell: Melissa, it starts by sharing our stories and that's why it's so important to remember and celebrate the story of Anita Hill. In your book, *Sister Citizen*, you talk about stories and through those stories, look at the barriers that women of color still face today. What was the impact on you personally of Anita Hill's courage and what are you seeing today that is a reflection of that important stand?

Melissa V. Harris-Perry: I feel a duality because I am a member of the academy and of media. In both realms we share stories and opinions and we talk . . . a lot. Because I'm married to an activist, I understand the difference between work that is on-the-ground and changes policy versus the sort of work I do.

Honestly, I can't believe it's been twenty years since Anita Hill testified at the Senate confirmation hearings of Clarence Thomas. It is a reminder of many different realities about where I am in my life right now. So let me indulge a bit by going back to where I was twenty years ago.

I was so excited to head off to college. But my freshman

year at a predominately white university proved challenging. I had some very negative experiences in the dorms. These were experiences shared among many of my African American girl-friends on campus. Many of us felt we didn't fit in. So at the end of our first year we founded a house on campus just for black women and named it Nia House. Nia means "purpose" in Swahili. It is the first organization that I was part of building from the very beginning. It was a house for African American women, fourteen of us choosing to live together and do pro-gramming around questions of cultural and racial purpose. We moved into that house together in August of 1991 and in October of 1991, we all sat together in our common area watching the Hill-Thomas hearings and confirmation.

By the time I had started college, I had already been sex-ually assaulted by my neighbor, an African American man. I already understood, in a very personal way what intrara-cial sexual violence is, but I didn't have any analytic lens to understand it. My mother spent her professional life in non-profit organizations and is an impressive, second-wave femi-nist and brilliant woman. So I certainly understood that the assault was not my fault. But I still didn't have any particular way of understanding the big politics around it, the ways that my personal experience connected to larger issues of power.

It is important to know that as I was sitting there watching the hearings in a house full of black women and processing the experience of my own sexual assault, I was a student at Wake Forest University. Wake Forest is also the academic home of Dr. Maya Angelou. At the same time that we were together as a group of women, watching Anita Hill testify, one of my dear, dear mentors, Professor Maya Angelou wrote a piece in the *New York Times* supporting Thomas. The piece was titled "I Dare to Hope" and basically made an argument that perhaps Thomas might prove to be a champion of racial interests after being appointed to and confirmed for the court. For those of us who were at Wake Forest University, that episode was a critical part of what had happened to us as we tried to process the events. And, for me, what the Hill testimony did was to start to help me understand analytically what my own experience of sexual assault had been, particularly intraracially.

I had developed enough of my racial consciousness at that point to understand interracial assault. But it wasn't until I read Dr. Angelou's piece that I had a sense of the power dynamics. The Hill hearings helped me understand how clearly African American women will be punished when we speak about sex in public, even if it's about our victimization around questions of sex. The Nia House was so important because it allowed us to watch, understand, and process it together. The Nia House became the beginning of all my academic work. The Angelou episode taught me that I would have dear African American mentors who would nonetheless see gender politics differently from me at various points.

In 1992, the next year, we watched Carol Moseley Braun get elected to the Senate from Illinois, largely as a result of the political activism that occurred after the hearings. Nineteen-ninety two was a triumphant moment for Democratic women, increasing the number of women in the House of Representatives. But then of course what happens in 1993? The vilification of Professor Guinier as a "quota queen." She was vilified within the Democratic Party as well as by her Republican opponents. Then in 2008, we have the election of the first African American President, this amazing and important moment, symbolically and substantively, and he brings

Joe Biden to the White House. Joe Biden, who behaved with such vitriol toward Hill in 1991 became the vice president to the first African American president.

In 2010, two years after this crazy win, domestic workers get their own win in New York with the passage of the Domestic Workers Bill of Rights. But in what seems like the very next moment, the most embraced book and film in America becomes *The Help*. I think of Ai-jen telling the story of women going to Arizona to listen to other women's stories and not becoming wealthy from those stories and not selling those stories as their own and not fantasizing or romanticizing or re-imagining their own position in those stories, but taking those stories and taking policy action, on behalf of the women. It's a total repudiation of the historical lie that is *The Help*. I feel twenty feet taller just listening to Ai-jen's stories, ones that engage in the questions of the realities of what it means to be a domestic worker in ways that actually impact women's lives. It's this kind of politics that I think we need to emphasize.

Going back to what Anita Hill means to me, Anita Hill means absolutely everything. Absolutely everything that I do, in terms of media and in terms of my work as a political scientist and even my own personal healing has its beginnings in October 1991.

Pat Mitchell: Rha Goddess, you are a performer who forces people to sit up and take notice. On a personal level, as you challenge people to go where they haven't gone before, to think beyond their own limitations, have you seen changes that began with Professor Hill?

Rha Goddess: It's complex. Women are all over the map right now in terms of how we understand and relate to our sense of feminine-hood and power.

In the fall of 1991, I was recently graduated from college and was working as an account representative for a Fortune 500 corporation in chemical sales. I was one of two African American women in the field. Growing up I had been well-schooled in understanding the politics and intraracial dynamics of gender in my community. But I was about to get a frontline education in the interracial dynamics of gender and power in the workplace. And unfortunately, these dynamics very often came under the guise of "mentorship."

As someone who was raised by parents born in the 1920s and who had survived over two decades of Jim Crow segregation, I had a very strong footing in the context of civil rights and social justice movements. The importance of what was happening with Clarence Thomas and Anita Hill was not lost on me.

I felt a deep sadness watching the hearings because the Supreme Court post Thomas was up for was vacant due to Thurgood Marshall's retirement. Marshall's legacy—as someone who fought tirelessly for justice and equality—was something to be proud of. What came to light in these hearings was not. I knew in the context of my own community that the hearings were going to create a battleground, whether it was in the beauty parlor or in the church parking lot; the debate and speculation over race versus gender would turn our community inside out. What has always stayed with me about Anita Hill is that she is someone who was willing to show great courage in the face of complexity: her willingness to stand up when nothing was guaranteed, not the support of her home base, not even the support of other black women; her willingness to say what is unpopular for truth's sake.

As an artist and activist I am especially aware of that legacy—to be willing to say what is unpopular and uncomfortable but true.

I have cut my teeth in the pioneering of speaking unpopular truth within the culture of hip hop and pop culture, and the fields of multimedia and entertainment. I am an empowered feminine voice in the face of an adopted tradition of misogyny which has been prevalent for many years in the commercial aspects of my art form—I have watched so many of my sisters struggle with their allegiance to the culture versus their own personal sense of dignity and self respect.

When I say it's complex, it's because we as women still have to navigate these issues in the realm of economic opportunity, and institutional leadership, and we have to navigate them in our personal relationships. Even where we feel that policy changes have happened, the cultural water is still contaminated with hostile attitudes and beliefs, and we're still drinking it. Some of us have had the strength and the courage to rise up against it. Some of us have had to grit our teeth and endure, very much like our mothers and our grandmothers and those who have come before. Some unfortunately have taken on distorted perceptions of what it means to speak the truth and have attempted to leverage it to their own advantage. And there are many of us who operate and struggle in the gray spaces of all of the above.

I believe our greatest opportunity today is to apply all we've learned, to use our feminine wisdom to help usher in this next iteration of the American Dream which includes the vision of a more just and sustainable world. As we re-imagine the American economy we see women's entrepreneurship rise in ways like never before and through this rise we get to redefine quality of life, work, and what it is to lead and do business with dignity, honor, and integrity for all. In this next generation of the dream, I see this as our moment as women. I believe every single one of us has something to contribute to a new brand of empowered citizens and to an ever growing "economy of transformation" which encourages the values of community, transparency, genuine accountability, and most of all, love.

I am thankful for Anita Hill's courageous contribution and humbled to be able to participate in this next chapter of cultural liberation for us all.

PAT MITCHELL is president and CEO of The Paley Center for Media, whose mission is to further understanding of media's role; past, present, and future. Mitchell began her media career three decades ago, as a news reporter, followed by posts as a White House correspondent, news anchor, contributor to NBC's *TODAY Show*, CBS's *Sunday Morning*, and other network and syndicated programs. She became the first woman to own and produce her own national talk-radio series, *Woman To Woman*, which won an Emmy. Mitchell's work as president of Turner Original Productions and CNN Productions was awarded multiple Emmy and Peabody awards, and two Academy Award nominations. In 2000, Mitchell became the first woman and first producer to become president and CEO of PBS. Among her many awards and recognitions for her professional and philanthropic work, Mitchell has received the Sandra Day O'Connor Award for Leadership, the Women in Cable and Telecommunications Woman of the Year Award, and was inducted into the Broadcasting & Cable Hall of Fame. Mitchell was named one of the 150 People Who Shake the World by *Newsweek* and one of the fifteen Powerful Women Over 50 by the *Huffington Post*. Most recently, she was honored with the inaugural Pat Mitchell Lifetime Achievement award by the Women's Media Center.

JOANNE N. SMITH is the founder and executive director of Girls for Gender Equity. Smith founded GGE in 2001 with the support of the Open Society Foundation to end gender-based violence and promote gender, race, and class equality. Smith is the co-author of *Hey Shorty: A Guide to Combating Sexual Harassment and Violence in Public Schools and on the Streets*. She has been honored by a number of prestigious organizations, has received the Union Square Award, been inducted into the New York City Hall of Fame, and received the Stonewall Women's Award from the Stonewall Democratic Club in recognition of her leadership and dedication to women's and LGBTQ rights. Recognized by her peers as a representative of the next generation of those who promote social justice and gender equality, Smith is part of the first Move to End Violence cohort—a ten-year initiative designed by NoVo Foundation to strengthen the collective capacity to end violence against girls and women in the United States.

AI-JEN POO is the director of the National Domestic Workers Alliance (NDWA), the leading voice for the nation's growing domestic workforce. She began organizing immigrant women workers in 1996 in the New York City Asian community. In 2000, she helped start Domestic Workers United (DWU), which led the way to the passage of the nation's first Domestic Workers Bill of Rights in 2010. After generations of exclusion, the breakthrough legislation extends labor protections to over two hundred thousand domestic workers in New York State. DWU helped to organize the first national meeting of domestic workers organizations, which resulted in the formation of the National Domestic Workers Alliance in 2007. She also serves as co-director of Caring Across Generations, a national initiative to create millions of new, quality jobs in home-based care, create pathways to citizenship and opportunity for care workers and support families in need of care as our nation ages. Among Ai-jen's numerous accolades are the Ms. Foundation Woman of Vision Award and the American Express NGen Leadership Award. In 2012, Ai-jen was included in *Newsweek*'s 150 Fearless Women in the World and *Time* magazine's 100 Most Influential People in the World.

EMILY MAY is an international leader in the movement against street-harassment. In 2005, at the age of twenty-four, she co-founded Hollaback! in New York City, and in 2010 she became its first full-time executive director. Hollaback!'s mission is to give women and LGBTQ folks an empowered response to street harassment, and ultimately, to end it. She argues that the Internet has provided new opportunities to tackle discrimination, by transforming discrimination from a lonely experience into a piece of a larger, public movement.

MELISSA V. HARRIS-PERRY is a professor of political science at Tulane University, where she is the founding director of the Anna Julia Cooper Project on Gender, Race, and Politics in the South. Harris-Perry is author of *Sister Citizen: Shame, Stereotypes, and Black Women in America* and the award winning *Barbershops, Bibles, and BET: Everyday Talk and Black Political Thought*. Harris-Perry is a columnist for the *Nation*, where she writes a monthly column also titled "Sister Citizen" and contributes to the group blog The Notion. She is the host of the *Melissa Harris-Perry Show* on MSNBC.

RHA GODDESS is a creative organizer, cultural innovator, and social entrepreneur who, for over thirty years, has worked on issues of racial justice and equality, electoral politics, offender aid and restoration, mental health and youth, and young women's empowerment. As a world-renowned performing artist and activist, her work has been internationally featured in several compilations, anthologies, forums, and festivals. Goddess is a 2008 recipient of the National Museum of Voting Rights prestigious Freedom Flame Award and a 2009 recipient of the Herb Alpert Award's Hedgebrook Prize. Also in 2009, Goddess was part of a special delegation invited to the White House and served as a US Cultural Envoy to Rwanda. In her latest venture Goddess is the founder and CEO of Move The Crowd, an entrepreneurial training company dedicated to helping the next generation stay true, get paid, and do good.

WORD POWER

HOPE ANITA SMITH

"It's been too hard living but I'm afraid to die
'Cause I don't know what's up there beyond the sky
It's been a long, a long time coming
But I know a change gon' come, oh yes it will"*

In the beginning
Was God
And long before He took a rib from
Adam's side
God gave Adam dominion
The Power to use his words . . .
I work.
I do my job.
Type, file, answer phones
Make a mean cup of coffee
But when the boss calls me into his office
I know my resume is lacking

*Lyrics to "A Change is Gonna Come" by Sam Cooke, 1964.

He runs his eyes up my skirt
Lingering a little too long on the assets
He did not find on my curriculum vitae.
His eyes are feeling me up
I try not to feel . . .
I am on the other side of the room
When he speaks
His words reach out like
tentacles
brush against my breasts
cup my behind.
When I look displeased
His mouth smiles and sends his words flying at
My face like the backside of a raised hand.
I feel the sting when he asks
"Do you like your job?
I want to say,
Be a man, just hit me.
He tells the joke about the woman who
Just couldn't get enough (if you know what I mean)
Wink, wink.
His words are erect
I open my mouth, take them in
I suck
in my breath
and
I swallow.
Laugh like I'm one of the guys
I've got two babies to feed
Rent to pay
And a car that occasionally runs.

There are days when
The weight of his words weighs heavy on me.
I can't get them off
I am pinned down
I can't move
I can't breathe
And I pray
I won't remember
This violation
This violence against me
the only evidence is viva voce
and there are no rape kits for words.
I don't want to testify
It's my word
Against his
My words are too small
I think how can I fight?
And the answer comes to me
how can I not?

My "no more" grabs him by the balls
Puts them in a vice grip
I take dictation and
Discover two new words
Slight and piddling
Humph
He's not so big
My words join hands
Gain courage and confidence as they hold on to each other
There is strength in numbers

The power of my words *cause* him to shrivel up
I word up
Reveal every bruise
Submit every dirty, slimy word that fondled, stroked, patted,
caressed, grazed, I say it again
No more.
And ladies,
Know more.
Know your place.
Know you have one.
And it's not on his lap
On your knees
Or lying prostrate across his desk
No more.
And no. I didn't ask for it
But it stops here
No more.
I may not win
But I will fight
I can't win if I don't fight
I win
Because I fight
I will be heard.

"There been times that I thought I wouldn't last for long
Now I think I'm able to carry on
It's been a long, a long time coming but I know
*A change gon' come, oh yes it will"**

*Lyrics to "A Change is Gonna Come" by Sam Cooke, 1964.

HOPE ANITA SMITH is the author of three books, including the award-winning *The Way A Door Closes*. Her second volume, *Keeping the Night Watch*, received the Coretta Scott King Honor. *School Library Journal* chose these titles as Best Books of the Year. Smith's third book, *Mother Poems*, which she wrote and illustrated, received the Myra Cohn Livingston Award for a distinguished book of poetry. Smith conducts writing workshops for children and adults writers of all ages using paint chips, found objects, magazine pictures, music, and food. She is a motivational speaker who loves to share her journey. She also conducts school assemblies that take her audience on a journey from idea to publication.

PART III

I STILL BELIEVE ANITA HILL

A POEM FOR ANITA HILL

KEVIN POWELL

This was written on the occasion of the twentieth anniversary of Ms. Hill's testimony at the Supreme Court hearings of Clarence Thomas in October 1991.

miss anita hill
what happens
when a woman
dares to split
her lips and
use the tongue
the universe
and the ancestors
gave her to
fingerpop the flesh
from lies
and expose
the truth
of a manhood
gone mad
?

miss anita hill
i thank you
as a man
for being
one of my teachers
for having the bottomless bravery
of sojourner truth
susan b. anthony
helen keller
ida b. wells
annie besant
frida kahlo
dorothy height
eleanor roosevelt
simone de beauvoir
fannie lou hamer
ella baker
audre lorde
angela davis
bella abzug
sonia sanchez
gloria steinem
susan taylor
alice walker
bell hooks
eve ensler
patti giggans
shelley serdahely
ani difranco
lynn nottage
debby tucker

april silver
dj kuttin kandi
dj beverly bond
cheyla mccornack
malia lazu
aishah shahidah simmons
laura dawn
pratibha parmar
maisha morales
richelle carey
blanca elizabeth vega
asha bandele
jessica care moore
my grandmother
my mother
my aunties
and all the women
whose names
we will never know
and all the women
who are not yet born

miss anita hill
do you know the
saga of my mother
a young woman
birthed from the scorn
of the old American South
oppressive Carolina clay of Jim Crow
hammered between her toes
with poverty and gloom

bookending the braided hair
of her youth—
first chance she got my ma
borrowed a greyhound
bus ride to freedom
worked odd jobs
like the one where
a rich man, a rich white man,
thought it his civic duty
to erase his skin of
everything except
his robe and his penis
sat on the synthetic sofa with
his legs wide open
so my mother could
see his private parts
they didn't call it
sexual harassment
back then in the early 1960s
they called it a job
and if you wanted
to keep that job
you had to scotch tape
the disgust gushing from
your throat and pretend
your womanhood had
not just been used
and discarded like a
soda can with pubic
hair spit-stuck to the rim

miss anita hill
what about my friend
who, just two weeks ago,
did the good deed of
checking on one of
the young people
from her youth program
because the girl's school
asked her to
little did my friend know
that she was moonwalking
into the den of
a dream deferred named stepfather
a poor man, a poor black man
he didn't like the questions
my friend was asking
him about the girl
so his manhood threw
kitchen chairs at my friend
like they were nuclear missiles
and when he had abused
those chairs he took the pieces
of the chairs and beat
my friend with those
when the pieces had
disintegrated in his hellish hands
he beat my friend with his fists
slapboxing with jesus
one rapper called it
except stepfather
wasn't jesus he was the devil—

a devil in redwhiteblue boxing trunks
and my friend an unwilling sparring partner
stepfather jabbed and sucker punched
my friend with body blows
beat her across the face
as her braces stabbed and
daggered the gums
of her mouth, the blood
bumrushing her brain the
way them busted levees
flooded new orleans in '05
miss anita hill, could
you hear her sorrow songs
for him to stop?
could you see the songs
of freedom in her black-and-blue eyes
as she slapboxed
with the devil, every hit
he gave she returned best she could
determined that her funeral
would not be in the rotted and ruined
home of a madman?
but stepfather beat my friend so bad
that the sixteen-year-old girl
stood upright and frozen
in the track marks of
her own nightmare
for three long years
stepfather had raped
this girl like it was
his divine order to do so
for three long years

stepfather had beaten
this girl like it was
his destiny to be a
domestic terrorist
9-1-1 the girl
called 9-1-1
to rescue not only my
friend but herself
she called 9-1-1
as stepfather slashed
and burned
my friend's clothes from her body
and readied his penis for invasion
the girl called 9-1-1
as my friend's mind and
bones were bodyslammed by trauma
and the greasy, sweat-stained floor
prepared itself for the receipt of her life
and it was right then that
the police came through the door—

miss anita hill
my friend spent a week
at a rape recovery center
she and that sixteen-year-old girl
I learned all of this
when my friend texted me
one day sharing what happened
she had been hung so high
from a shock
tree that she could not remember if
it happened on a

thursday or friday
but it was one of those
days, she was sure
miss anita hill
the stepfather is in
jail now and that girl
has been freed from her
prison
just the way
you've liberated so many
women and girls
from manmade boxes
twenty long years ago
simply by having the audacity to
set sexism on fire
miss anita hill
have you ever thought
of how many women
and girls would not
be free now if
your voice had
not freed them?
you are like harriet tubman
your life
the underground railroad
that has taken
so many to a place
they did not know existed

and when the
closing chapters of your

life are penciled into the moon
miss anita hill
they will say
that you were a human
being a woman
a black woman
a sister a friend
a leader
a mentor
a teacher who
they tried to mock and malign
and crush and defeat
who they
said did not see
what she saw
did not feel what she felt
but who because of the
convictions in her
lone tree, oklahoma soul
got up anyway
because that is
what the selfless do
they martyr
even their own
sanity their own lives
and in so doing
they know they
birth a child called change
a new birth day
a new v-day
where women and girls

like you, miss anita hill
like my mother
like my grandmother
and my aunts
like my friend
and that sixteen-year-old girl
and all the women
and girls whose names
we will never know
can say I too can be
free I too can use
my power and my voice
because miss anita hill
said so—

KEVIN POWELL is a writer, activist, and public speaker. He is the author or editor of eleven books, including his latest, *Barack Obama, Ronald Reagan, and The Ghost of Dr. King: Blogs and Essays.*

WHAT DOES CREDIBILITY LOOK LIKE?

PATRICIA J. WILLIAMS

When Anita Hill's first book *Speaking Truth to Power* came out, I interviewed her for an article in *Harpers*. One of the things she mentioned was her anxiety about the moment she had to walk from backstage into the Congressional hearing room and onto the national stage. She described her feelings in a way I found quite poignant. She said, "The only thing I could think of was 'am I wearing the right thing?'"

I could relate to that anxiety. Anita and I began our careers back in the caveman years of the legal profession. She's younger than I, but we're approximately the same age in terms of the women's movement and its incredible paroxysms around what we could wear or not wear. Anita and I lived through the era of dressed-for-success suits; those little getups with two matching pieces—a big shouldered jacket with A-line skirt—in black or navy blue only. Occasionally some of us wore gray, but it was—and still may be—against protocol to wear gray when arguing before the Supreme Court. You also had to have the regulation low-heeled pumps; those blouses with the big flouncy bows at the throat, which were supposed to be the equivalent of men's ties; button earrings; and maybe, if you were really extravagant, a thick rope of pearls.

So when Anita Hill put on that sky blue outfit for her testimony, it was something of a departure. It was as though some of the old guard might be blinded by the intensity of optometric wavelength. That suit—so simple and conservative by any measure—nevertheless resonated in a way that I'm not sure younger women can appreciate in today's world, even though it is certainly true that the angst over what to wear is just as common as it ever has been. After all, we recently witnessed the agonizing cross-examination of Hillary Clinton about whether a pantsuit was an appropriate coat of armor. Or the anxiety about Michelle Obama choosing to bare her legs and arms. Similarly, before Elena Kagan became a Supreme Court justice, she was solicitor general of the United States. And I don't know if you're aware, but the official outfit for the Solicitor General had always been a morning coat. Yes, a morning coat. You know, what gentlemen royals wear to Ascot? That coat with the tails and the pinstriped trousers? Needless to say, there was some apprehension about whether Elena Kagan would have to don a bustle and crinoline.

In any event, the real question underlying Anita Hill's self-interrogation was not about "wearing the right thing." Rather, it was an expression of that still-much-too-familiar anxiety: What does credibility look like? What does a woman have to wear to be believed?

But we are here today to ask a different question. Who is Anita Hill, regardless of her choices—elegant though they may be—of what to wear? What we know from her bio is that she graduated from the University of Oklahoma undergraduate and from Yale Law School in 1980; and that she was put into the relentlessness of that frenzied media spotlight in 1991. But there is a back history to her story, because it did not take Clarence Thomas to make her a pioneer or a heroine.

When Anita began teaching in 1983, there were virtually no women or women of color teaching anywhere in the United States. I'm not sure of the precise numbers in 1983, but in 1980 there were exactly six women of color in legal academia in the entire country. There were four African Americans, one Latina, one Asian American woman—and that statistic includes the historically black law schools.

Anita Hill became the first tenured African American, as well as the first tenured African American woman, at the University of Oklahoma's School of Law. And before her teaching career she also served as an advisor to the assistant secretary of education, as well as to the chair of the Equal Opportunity Employment Commission.

In November of 1995, she wrote *Speaking Truth to Power*, which could be described as memoir, but it is much more than that. It is a detailed coming-of-age story of the entire women's movement; and it is a thorough, lucid, and beautifully written exposition of the law of sexual harassment. I highly recommend it.

Today, Anita Hill is professor of social policy, law and women's studies at Brandeis University, and she also serves as senior advisor to the provost there. In 2011, she published *Reimagining Equality: Stories of Gender, Race and Finding Home,* a riveting account of the impact that the housing crisis has had on women.

In short, Anita Hill is an enormously accomplished woman. The scope of her career is both broad and deep. We do her an injustice if we freeze her in time as an icon of the hearings, or the symbol of a single event. Her words and independent achievements must not be overshadowed by Clarence Thomas's words, which are continually being written into history. We must take her scholarship very seriously, for she is immensely and uniquely insightful. That means we must do our homework and cite her articles and read her books, rather than just using her as the deus ex machina for a conversation about gender. As important as that is, we must also listen to the substance of what she has contributed to the law and to the world.

PATRICIA J. WILLIAMS writes the monthly column "Diary of a Mad Law Professor" for the *Nation*. Her writing covers broad issues of social justice, including the rhetoric of the war on terror, race, ethnicity, gender, all aspects of civil rights law, bioethics and eugenics, forensic use of DNA, and comparative issues of class and culture in the US, France, and Britain. Her book, *The Alchemy of Race and Rights*, was named one of the twenty-five best books of 1991 by the *Voice Literary Supplement*. Williams is also the James L. Dohr Professor of Law at Columbia University. She is the recipient of numerous honorary degrees; an Alumnae Achievement Award from Wellesley College; the Graduate Society Medal from Harvard; and of the MacArthur Foundation's so-called "Genius" Grant. As a law professor, she has testified before Congress, acted as a consultant and coordinator for a variety of public interest lawsuits and served as a past member of the Boards of the Center for Constitutional Rights; The Society of American Law Teachers; and of the National Organization for Women's Legal Defense and Education Fund.

GIVE YOUR CHILD YOUR LUGGAGE, NOT YOUR BAGGAGE

ANITA F. HILL

Many of you have this vision or image of me sitting in that Senate room by myself in front of that long table with all of the senators lined up facing me. But I want to remind you that I also had some wonderful people who, as they say, had my back, and who came together because they believed in the process. They believed in the integrity of the court, as I did, and they wanted to make sure that I could be fairly treated as best as they could help me.

Many of the people who came together were my colleagues in teaching. There were so few of us in teaching law and these wonderful individuals, including Judith Resnik, who knew me as a student at Yale Law School, joined my team. People talk about our hotshot team, and it was. But it wasn't that high-powered law firm that people liked to make it out to be.

Twenty years is a long time to keep people together. The people who were on that team in the beginning are still with me. The witnesses, Ellen Wells, Sue Hoerchner, John Carr and Joel Paul, who were friends of mine back in the early eighties, are still friends of mine today. I have been very fortunate not only to keep those people in my life, but also to engage with supporters throughout these last twenty years, who have made what I do and my survival possible.

There are all kinds of pressure that are put on someone who has gone through these kinds of claims or attempted to correct problems. And of course you have to know that you can lose people along the way.

I had lots of support from women, and there were so many men that helped, as well. For instance, John Frank had come from Arizona as an individual to volunteer. He was an expert on the Supreme Court. I didn't even know he was going to come to the hearings. At the end of my morning testimony, he said to me in tears, literally in tears, "I know this is hard for you. I know this is a challenge. But you have no idea how important this is to our country."

At that point, I was just trying to get through the rest of the day, and I don't think I fully appreciated exactly what he was saying to me. But here was this man who had been at Yale many years ago, had practiced law, and studied the Supreme Court, and he was saying to me that this was an important moment in our country's history. It was as though he had looked into the future and saw today, preparing me for what was to come.

It was a testament to people like Frank and to my friends that I was able to continue on after the hearings. There was pressure at the University of Oklahoma for me to be fired. It was coming from officials, legislators, state legislators. When that didn't work, there were threats to the law school, and to the existence of the law school. And, of course, there was an effort for my colleagues to turn against me.

It was very difficult because this testimony had become an event. Immediately after the hearing, polling showed that seventy percent of the population thought that I had perjured myself. Going to the grocery store, I realized that seven out of the ten people that I would encounter there thought that I had perjured myself in my testimony. In addition to the pressures that I was having on the job, there were threats against me personally, bomb threats at the law school and at my home.

A week or so after I gave testimony, and the vote was taken, I wanted to say, "It's over. Enough is enough. I want my life back." And I remember resenting the fact that I couldn't get it back, that it wasn't coming back the way I thought it had been. Once I let go of that idea and thought, You know what? It's not going to happen that way. I have a different life now. With that realization I had to ask myself: What life do I want now? I could accept that it wasn't going to be the life that I had. It was a pretty good life and I liked it, but I knew it wasn't going to be the same ever again. And so I had to figure out, What can I shape and claim for myself so that I can continue to be productive, to do the things that I care about, and to continue to live.

I had to assess what my resources were, what my talents were, what could I do and what were my options and possibilities. What kind of support was I going to get as I moved on in life? Those were all things that I had to sit down and account for and at least I had a chance to shape it. But the other thing that I had to do was to say, "You know what? This was an event. This was an important event. It has helped to shape my life. But it is just an event. It's not me. It's not who I am." And so I had to understand who I am and understand why I was on this earth in order to move forward.

When I look back at my own family's stories, I realize that who I was had so much to do with how I was raised. When my grandparents homesteaded eighty acres in Arkansas in 1895 it was a significant milestone in our family achievement. That my grandfather had gone from being property, having been born a slave, to owning property was significant. They lost that farm in circumstances that were not unlike what's going on today: bad credit options, a poor economy, then there was an agricultural economy, racial unrest and violence. It had an impact on my mother and our entire family. And I think the same is true for young people today. This home insecurity will, indeed, impact their future and their present, for instance, whether or not they're able to get student loans through their parents.

When I was writing *Reimagining Equality*, I wanted to tell a story of the significance of home without really having to tell it through the lens of male domination. I wanted to tell it through the eyes of women. The assumption is that the home includes two parents and children; and the assumption is that those two parents are a man and a woman. That's how we've thought about the home and home policy, but as we look at who the new home buying market was in 2005, we learn that a lot of women were buying on their own. For me the significance is not just for women on their own, but also for their children in the next generation.

When the housing crisis hit, the collapse of the market devastated communities and sent so many people into chaos. But when I read the stories in the press, so few of those reported include the impact that it was having on women, especially women of color; women living on their own and trying to buy homes on their own. What I realized was that the housing crisis is not only a setback economically, it is a setback in our social advances for women because women weren't out there buying homes on their own for the last twenty years. This ability to buy homes was a social advancement for women because we were finally saying, we don't have to wait until we have a spouse or a partner. We can go out on our own. That was an important movement that was occurring in the year 2005.

When we think about stories like *A Raisin in the Sun* or in popular culture, *The Jeffersons*, the home is such a significant feature for African Americans' equality. In order to show that the Jeffersons had made it, what did they do? They moved on up to the Upper East Side. And it wasn't just any place in the Upper East Side. It was the deluxe apartment in the sky. And as the theme song goes, "They didn't even eat the same food anymore." When Louise Jefferson "made it," she becomes a stay-at-home mother and gets a black maid.

What I really enjoyed about writing my latest book is that it brings together so many parts of my life. It brings together my life as a teacher. It brings together my life as a granddaughter of a slave, a great-granddaughter of a woman who was a single mother for ten years when she moved from slavery to being a free person, even though she lived in a slave cabin for those first ten years. It brings together my history. It brings together some of the impact that the hearings had on me. And it really brings me to the issue of equality that I care about. Sexual harassment is one of those issues. What I try to do in this book is to give voice to the people who have not been heard from during this crisis. And that's really what I've been trying to do with the issue of sexual harassment for the past twenty years; to help people find their voices, to talk about the issues that keep them from living their lives fully and as equals.

I once had a conversation with the wonderful filmmaker Ken Burns. It was a moving conversation for me because, he too had grown up during the civil rights era and also lost his mother at a young age. Naturally, this was a very emotional time in his life and has been a part of his storytelling. When he created his trilogy—*The Civil War, Baseball* and *Jazz*—he said he did so because each of those were metaphors about race in America. I found that moving and initially I thought it made sense. But then I thought further and most of the stories of the Civil War, jazz music, and baseball capture only male experiences. With the baseball series, there was one segment about the women's league that formed during and after World War II. So my question to him was, "Well, if there is a metaphor for race, is there a way for us to think and talk about race that isn't so male dominated?" What conversation do we have about race that includes women?"

His response was, "Well, I did the piece on Susan B. Anthony and Elizabeth Cady Stanton to talk about gender." And I said, "Well, that's problematic because as we know, in the suffrage movement, there was marginalization of African American women. So how do we then have a conversation about gender that is not racialized?"

From there I started thinking about ways to do that. What is our metaphor for thinking about equality that doesn't rely on male domination or racialization? How can we have an inclusive conversation about equality? There is one element that looms large in our quest for equality and that is home. The finding of a home and the establishing of a place that one calls their own. That's why I included home in the title of my latest book.

This leads to my twenty-first-century vision of equality. In the final chapter, "Home at Last: Toward an Inclusive Democracy," I present three definitions of home. "Home is a lens through which one can safely view the world." This is significant because we know that for so many women, space inside the home is not a safe space. And it is an important element for us to have that home from which we can view the world safely. The second part of the definition is "A place where one's ideas, experience, and work are seen as valuable." That, for me, symbolizes so much of what is missing in the lives of women: valuing our work, whatever it might be. We are trying to be valued for who we are and what we have to offer, not only our work, but our ideas and experiences. Finally, I say that "home is an ideal state of being as much as a place, which is re-imagined for each generation."

My great-grandmother had to imagine what freedom was like after living her life as a slave. She had to imagine what freedom was like for herself and her son, my grandfather. My mother, when she sent me away to college in the 1970s, into a world that she had no understanding of, she had to imagine what equality was going to be like for me. She had to help me imagine because it was not her experience, having been born in 1911. She didn't know what the world was going to be like.

When I was seventeen years old, my mother said to me, "I want you to come with me. We are going to visit a family friend." This family friend was a teacher, an African American woman, who had taught some of my siblings English. She had traveled widely in her life, but now she was older and sick and no longer able to travel. She said she had something that she wanted to give me: a set of brown Samsonite luggage, with her initials on them. Four years later, as I was heading off to law school, my mother gave me a gift: my own brand-new set of Samsonite luggage that my mother had saved S&H Green Stamps to get. My mother sent me off to law school with two sets of luggage, the older version and now my own set with my own initials pasted on. The symbolism of both of those women, who were sending me out into a world that was going to be so different from their own and the courage that each of them had to say, "Okay, I have prepared you. I have given you something. Go out. Claim your own life. Claim your own home and be all that you can be." I think about it today when people ask, "Well, what's the best gift you ever received?" And I say, "It was those two sets of luggage and what they symbolized for me." So, I would say, "Give your daughters luggage." As my friend, Kathleen says, "Give them luggage and not baggage."

My mother had to imagine for herself and her children what equality was going to be like. I think we're at that juncture now. We must imagine, for a new generation, what equality is going to be like. We have reached the point now, for example, when we say sexual harassment, we can raise our voices and we can complain about it. But we should imagine a workplace where it no longer exists. When we talk about the events that are going on in the world and the issues we are struggling with today, for instance, the occupation of Wall Street, all of us are trying to imagine what equality is going to be like in the twenty-first century.

ANITA HILL, the youngest of thirteen children from a farm in rural Oklahoma, received her JD from Yale Law School in 1980. She began her career in private practice in Washington, DC, with a focus on banking law and litigation. Before becoming a law professor, she worked as an advisor to the assistant secretary of the US Education Department and the chairman of the Equal Employment Opportunity Commission. In 1989, Hill became the first African American to be tenured at the University of Oklahoma, College of Law. Hill continues her teaching and research. Hill recently became of counsel at Cohen, Milstein, Sellers, and Toll. She is the author of *Speaking Truth to Power*, a memoir, and *Reimagining Equality: Stories of Gender, Race, and Finding Home*. Hill is a senior advisor to the provost and professor of social policy, law, and women's studies at Brandeis University.

But what's all this here talking about? Just thought I'd reach out to ask you across the airwaves and the years, Anita Hill, and ask you to consider something. Anita Hill, please don't tell nobody, no how, nowhere, never, no way that you're sorry. Anita Hill, please don't you apologize chile. Because for one thing: you told the truth. (Don't you just love that play on my name?) Yes, my dear, being called Truth myself, I know indeed you told the truth. All of us here in the ancestral world, the foremothers as you all call us now. (Watch out one day y'all will be foremothers yourselves and it has a way of making you feel old, don't it?) But I digress, as you all might say. In any case, Anita Hill, no one on God's earth should ever have to, or be asked to apologize for telling the truth. Besides, Anita Hill, did anyone else take—what's this they call it? [member of audience calls out "lie detector test"]. That's right, folks think I've not been following all this—but did anyone else take a lie detector test and pass it but you, Anita Hill? Another thing Anita Hill: no one has ever apologized to you. No one has ever apologized to you for dragging your name through the mud. For calling you a pawn, a woman scorned. No one has ever apologized to you Anita Hill for your, what's this he called it? [member of audience calls out "high-tech lynching"]. No one has ever apologized to you Anita Hill for your . . .high-tech lynching. . . as a black woman who deigned to think for herself. So Anita Hill, honey, please never, no way, no how nowhere ever say you're sorry. Please child, don't apologize. Because if you apologize— you'll think I haven't been following all this—if you apologize, then we might all be asked to apologize, me and Abigail Adams and Susan B. Anthony and the whole lot of us. Even our dear sister Harriet Tubman might be asked to apologize. What silliness! What foolishness! What arrogance. You mean to tell me that stuff is still happening 'round here. Folks asking us to apologize for telling what we've seen, what folks have done to us, what we've endured, what we've done suffered. What foolishness indeed. And you know what honey, if you apologize, all these little girls out here might be asked to apologize too each time someone they work for ask them out and they say hell no. They will have to apologize for—-what's this they call it? Work notes [member of audience calls out "evaluations"]. They will have to apologize for bad work evaluations that they don't deserve. (Y'all don't think I haven't been following all this and catching the lingo.) These girls and women out here will have to apologize for what they wear, for where they walk, how they talk—especially if they talk like me. They'd have to apologize for who they are, free women who work, who speak, who true to my name, tell the truth. So please don't apologize Anita Hill because if you apologize—y'all might not think I've been following all this, but I have—if you apologize Anita Hill, Nafissatou Diallo and every woman like her, in the same situation as her, Tristane Banon and every woman like her and every woman in the same situation as her, might be asked to apologize to the International Monetary Fund and to—what's this they call him [member of audience calls out "DSK"]. Yes, these women might be asked to apologize to all the freaking DSKs of the world. That's right honey. So please don't apologize Anita Hill because if you apologize Lois Jenson and the women of the Eveleth Taconite Minnesota mine might be asked to apologize for filing the first class action sexual harassment suit in this here country. (Oh Susan B. sure like that one.) If you apologize, Anita Hill, Paula Puopolo might be asked to apologize to the secretary of the navy and the two hundred sailors who attacked her at the Tailhook convention. (My friend Elizabeth Blackwell followed that one closely with us.) How far would it have to go, Anita Hill, if you apologize? As Susan B.

is always telling us out here, the older you get, the greater the power you'll have to help the world. You're like a snowball, Susan B. like to say, and it sure is true for you Anita Hill. You're like a snow ball, chile, the further you are rolled, the more strength you will gain. And the more strength you gain, the stronger we all get and you prove to us that all the work we did, all the marching, all the writing, is not in vain. I hope Anita Hill that the years, though surely not easy, have already proven that to you, Anita Hill. Susan B. is asking me to ask how come everyone's not all on fire? She say she believe she'll explode if some of you don't wake up. So please don't tell nobody nowhere, no way no how, that you are sorry, Anita Hill. [Speaker recites along with Anita Hill's voice this final paragraph from her opening statement at the hearing.] "It would have been more comfortable to remain silent. But I [speaker says you] felt you had to tell the truth. I [speaker says you] could not keep silent." You don't need to be sorry for not being silent, Anita Hill. Susan B. jus told me to tell you that again. You don't never need to apologize for that. You don't need to give it any more thought, Anita Hill, or pray on it. Those who need your forgiveness can pray for it themselves. I hope this will never be asked of you again. Obliged to you for hearing me, Anita Hill. Very much obliged.

SOUND OF PHONE HANGING UP. STAGE GOES DARK.

EDWIDGE DANTICAT is the author of numerous books, including *Breath, Eyes, Memory*; *Krik? Krak!*, a National Book Award finalist; *The Farming of Bones*, an American Book Award winner; and *The Dew Breaker*, a PEN/ Faulkner Award finalist and winner of the first Story Prize.

PART IV

WHAT HAVE WE LEARNED
IN TWENTY YEARS,
AND WHAT COMES NEXT?

THE BLOODLESS COUP

DEBORAH COPAKEN KOGAN

My teenage daughter showed up to my Orthodox Jewish father-in-law's funeral in a striped miniskirt and shit-kicker boots. It couldn't be helped. The black dress I'd bought her two years earlier as my young father lay dying no longer fit, while Maurice, my ninety-five-year-old father-in-law, was here one minute, gone the next, which left no time to shop.

Jews being Jews, especially Orthodox Jews being Orthodox Jews, Maurice's body had to be buried within twenty-four hours, in a plot he'd reserved from a sect called Moriah—spelled M-O-R-I-A-H but pronounced as in "How do you solve a problem like. . .?" The Moriah used to run an Orthodox shul on the Upper West Side above Zabar's, which my father-in-law joined after a decade spent hiding from Nazis. He purchased the plot almost immediately after arriving in America because while Hitler was dead, you never knew with Nazis.

Hours after Maurice took his final breath, a Moriah representative contacted my mother-in-law to remind her that women, as per their misinterpretation of Halachic law, would not be allowed at the gravesite. This was not wholly unexpected news to the grieving widow, but it was also, under the circumstances, not the most welcome news either. Her current rabbi—who like the majority of Jews, even the most orthodox, believes that shoveling dirt onto the deceased provides a necessary first step in the mourning process—was called upon to try to broker a better deal. The negotiations between the two sides lasted well into the night, at which point the Moriah rabbi finally broke down and agreed that the female mourners could accompany the body to the cemetery, so long as we remained hidden in the cars until the grave was three-quarters filled. We were told it had something to do with the possibility of contaminating the corpse with menstrual blood, although try as I might, I was unable to form a mental image of how such a defiling would occur without imagining scenes better suited to fetish porn.

The next morning, during the ride from the funeral home to the cemetery, I was sitting in the back seat with my two eldest children when I realized that I'd neglected to inform them of the whole girls-have-to-hide-in-the-car-until-the-grave's-three-quarters-full deal. So I told them.

"What are we, in the Stone Age?" said my then fifteen-year-old son. My daughter could barely speak, the look on her face hovering somewhere between disbelief and the kind of rage for which animal tranquilizers were invented. Then it hit me: here was a girl, or rather a woman by Jewish law, who was born into an era in which she'd never rubbed up against the absurdities of sexism. Never. She'd never been told, as my mother once had, that only the boys in the family could go to medical school. Her right to vote has always been sacrosanct. Her school cannot claim they have no money for girls' sports. No male superior will ever be able to ask, "Who's put a pubic hair on my Coke?" without serious repercussions. "But that's ridiculous!" she said. "I know," I said, "It is. But that's the deal that was struck, so we have to stick to it." At the cemetery, framed through the window of our car, a waddle of black-suited men encircled my father-in-law's grave, first rocking back and forth in prayer, then doing the hard manual labor of burial. I tried to distract my daughter from her anger with stories about her grandfather. "Remember the time you were five, and he asked you what your favorite sandwich was, and you said, 'Proscuitto and brie?' and then Grandma said, 'That's not kosher,' and you said, 'What's kosher?'"

My mother-in-law reminisced about the morning, two decades earlier, when Maurice had belted out the Marseillaise while being wheeled down the hallway for the surgery no one thought he'd survive. My sister-in-law told stories of her father's imprisonment in plain sight during the Holocaust, how he learned to take communion and say, "Bless me father, for I have sinned," without sounding like an imposter. I wondered if anyone else was noticing the irony of our own imprisonment, sixty years later, in the back of that car. How complacently we wore the armbands of our gender without ripping them to shreds.

Finally, from our hidden vantage point, the grave appeared to be three-quarters full, give or take a sixteenth, so we women—about forty of us, many wearing the modest long skirts and post-matrimonial head coverings typical of orthodox women—stepped out of the car and started walking toward the mound of earth. Which is when the white-bearded rabbi appeared, seemingly out of nowhere.

"What are you doing?" shouted the rabbi, now running toward us, shooing us back in the car, physically blocking all those uteri from getting any nearer to the grave. "This is a disgrace! Get back in the car! Back in the car!" Clearly, no one had told him about the deal. My mother-in-law started to cry. The other women were shocked into silence.

Which is when my daughter, all miniskirted four-feet-ten of her, clomped up to the rabbi in her shit-kicker boots and said, "Excuse me, sir, but my grandmother would like to bury her husband. We had a deal. Now, please, move out of the way."

Without looking back, she pushed her way past the rabbi and marched those boots straight toward the mound of dirt, where she yanked the shovel out of my husband's hand and thrust it deep into the earth. The rest of us women stood there, immobilized, not knowing how to proceed. Little Norma Rae could ostensibly be forgiven. Yes, she was thirteen, but she looked no older than ten. Her uterus, one presumed—or at least one presumed the rabbi was presuming—wasn't yet shedding its lining. "Come on!" she shouted, urging us on with her hand.

The rabbi from the cemetery stood his ground. "Get back in the car," he told us. "This is a DISGRACE!"

My daughter leaned on the shovel, her tiny frame dwarfed by it.

Seeing her standing there, armed for battle amid that sea of black, I took my mother-in-law's hand in mine, and we made a wide detour around the rabbi. My sisters-in-law followed. A few seconds later, the entire amoeba of long-skirted women meandered its way toward the grave. Our bloodless coup was complete. We grabbed some shovels and started digging.

DEBORAH COPAKEN KOGAN is a best-selling author of *Shutterbabe*, a memoir, and the novels *Between Here and April* and *The Red Book*.

She has contributed to The Moth and the Six-Word Memoir storytelling series, and has written for *Financial Times*, the *New York Times*, the *New Yorker*, among others. A former award-winning photojournalist, covering conflicts in areas such as Afghanistan, Romania, Israel, Zimbabwe, and the former Soviet Union, her photographs appeared in newspapers and magazines worldwide. She produced TV news for ABC News, where she won an Emmy, as well as for NBC News, and CNN.

SEVERE AND PERVASIVE

KATHLEEN PERATIS

I'm a lawyer, a long-time practitioner of employment discrimination law, and a partner at Outten and Golden LLP in New York City. I guess I am what Arlen Spector and others disparage by calling a "slick lawyer," a way to put down those who are passionate about justice. The work is hard and in Anita's day even more so than today, claimants were so far ahead of the times that they were often unsuccessful in their legal claims. The law was so inhospitable in the 1990s and for many years thereafter that had Anita brought a legal claim—which she never did—it is likely that she would have lost in a court of law.

At about the same time as Anita Hill claims exploded onto the public scene, my firm was involved in a very similar case, unsuccessful at the trial stage and then successful on appeal, which is why I am able to speak publicly about it. The details of this case give you a flavor of what the law was like in 1991.

The claimant was a woman named Lisa Petrosino who worked for Bell Atlantic, which is now Verizon, repairing telephone lines. She worked out of a garage in Staten Island with an all-male crew who tormented her every day. The banter among the men in the workplace was crude and misogynistic, which would have been bad enough for Lisa, but they also singled her out. They drew crude pictures of headless women, women with their legs spread in the air, pictures of men having sex with animals, and of her having sex with supervisors, and left them in terminal boxes she was assigned to work on so she would find them. She felt threatened by the depictions of dismembered women. She said, "It's not that I don't have a sense of humor, but this stuff is not funny." They ridiculed her appearance, they told her to "calm her big tits," they said she complained because she was "on the rag." Bell Atlantic not only did nothing to stop it, their supervisors joined in. Bell Atlantic's lawyers, one of whom was a woman, argued that none of this was illegal, it was just boys being boys. The federal district court judge agreed with them and dismissed the case.

The Supreme Court had decided years before that sexual harassment and hostile environment were illegal, but the prejudices of the trial judges remained. In Lisa's case, the trial judge saw no illegality. The appellate court finally reversed and sent the case back to the trial court for trial, and at that point, the case was settled. So the wrong was righted, in a way, but only in a way. Like Anita, Lisa suffered greatly along that road to justice.

Some women are transformed by the vindication of a legal victory but some find the process totally debilitating and demoralizing. Women who go public still get punished. It's a sad reality, but some of my happiest clients are the ones who settled for less than their claim was worth and even the ones who decided not to complain at all. Women were punished in 1991, they were punished in 2000, and the sad reality is they are punished still today. I was recently retained by a woman who works at a major education institution in New York City. She was having a business dinner with her boss and he put her hand on his crotch, on his erect penis, freaking her out. She will probably sue and it will be harder on her than she can imagine. These cases do happen less now than they used to but when it happens to you, that is cold comfort.

But let me tell you a little bit about what is actually illegal, then and now. The definition of an illegal hostile environment has not changed—it is an environment where there is an atmosphere of hostility and misogyny that is either severe or pervasive. These words are subject to interpretation, of course, but in most courts, "severe" means that the bad actor, as we call him in my business, has engaged in at least some unwanted or unwelcome touching. I will explain the "unwanted" part in a minute. As for the "touching," it doesn't have to be rape, but to have a really good case for hostile environment discrimination it has to be serious. In the absence of unwanted touching, the claimant has to show that the bad actions were pervasive, and that means a pattern of incidents. How many? No one can quantify what is enough and as in any legal case, it will depend on many things, such as how the claimant and the other witnesses come across to this particular judge or jury.

I mention that the conduct has to be "unwelcome." This is very important because it provides defendants with the opportunity to blame the victim by saying she was a willing participant. It is the "You asked for it" defense. "Why did you send your boss birthday cards or light-hearted emails, if you were bothered by his conduct?" "Why did you get drunk at the holiday party?" "Why did you let your boss come to your room when you were traveling?" "Why did you tell all those off-color jokes?" "Why did you wear a skirt so short, if you're not a slut?" "Why didn't you quit?"

Because this road is so tough, I often hear clients say, "Why me? Why did this have to happen to me? Why has my life been turned upside down by this creep who had no right to do this to me?" And it is unfair. But the law has been transformed by the many women who have bravely stepped up and paved the way for the rest of us. That is what Anita did. With courage and guts, she changed everything.

KATHLEEN PERATIS, co-chair of the Sex, Power, and Speaking Truth: Anita Hill 20 Years Later conference, is a partner and member of the executive committee at the New York law firm Outten and Golden LLP, where she chairs its public interest and sexual harassment practice groups. She has represented hundreds of survivors of workplace discrimination and abuse. She is the founding chair of the Women's Right Division of Human Rights Watch. She has been honored as a Super Lawyer and as one of New York Area's Best Lawyers by *New York* magazine.

STUNNED BUT NOT BOWED

KIMBERLE WILLIAMS CRENSHAW

*"What holds communities of struggle together are the
collective memories. We give life and validity to our
constructions of race, gender, class, community and politics
by giving those constructions a history."*

*"Central to constructing more radical political struggles
is the reclamation and reconstruction of fuller, more
complex histories."*[1]

The lasting image that would forever represent the rebellious
moment that gave rise to the Anita Hill-Clarence Thomas
hearings featured seven fiercely determined members of the
House of Representatives storming the Senate.[2] Elected representatives though they were, there was another commonality
that drove them to rebel—they were women, each outraged that

1. Elsa Barkley Brown, "Imaging Lynching: African American Women, Communities of Struggle, and Collective Memory," in *African American Women Speak Out
On Anita Hill-Clarence Thomas*, ed. Geneva Smitherman (Detroit, MI: Wayne State
University Press; 1995), 121.
2. See Maureen Dowd, "The Thomas Nomination: 7 Congresswomen March
to Senate to Demand Delay in Thomas Vote," *New York Times*, Oct. 9, 1991, A1.
Included were Barbara Boxer (California); Nita M. Lowey (New York); Patsy T. Mink

their colleagues in the Senate had cavalierly dismissed credible evidence of sexual harassment by a Supreme Court nominee. Their refusal to accept what was conventional and safe became the predicate for—indeed the foundation of—a wide cultural shift in how sexual power in the workplace is conceived. Beyond the specific matter of sexual harassment, the siting of the rebellion on the Capitol steps fueled a widespread discourse about the underrepresentation of women in Congress, prompting a concerted effort to storm the halls of power more permanently. Indeed, as the twentieth-year commemoration of Anita Hill's courageous testimony unfolded, perhaps the most celebrated aspect of this historical moment is its foundational role in shifting the discursive terrain about sexual harassment and women and political power.

There were of course, other moments of rebellion that the hearings prompted, moments that will never enjoy the iconic status of the "Boxer rebellion." These moments fall outside of the rituals of collective memory in part because the conceptual plane upon which they were staged remains incomprehensible within the prevailing lenses through which gender and race politics are framed and understood. Despite its disruptive action, the "Boxer rebellion" was made meaningful within an existing interpretive frame of "women" objecting to an all-too-typical pattern of "male" disregard of matters thought to be important to "women." This narrative in turn helps to highlight and indeed, crystallize a prevailing interpretation of what was at stake—women talking

---

(Hawaii); Eleanor Holmes Norton (nonvoting delegate, District of Columbia); Patricia Schroeder (Colorado); Louise Slaughter (New York); Jolene Unsoeld (Washington). For how the strategy of storming the Senate displayed by this group of elected officials has been replicated since, see also Chad Pergram, "A Foray Behind Enemy Lines," *Fox News*, June 6, 2012, http://politics.blogs.foxnews.com/2012/06/06/foray-behind-enemy-lines.

back to power. As this framing is remembered and retold to new generations of gender activists, the narratives that it foregrounds reproduce the political rhetorics that that snapshot engendered.

Another rebellion was also ignited by Anita Hill's courageous testimony, a fierce resistance to a particular kind of intraracial power made up of a set of learned expectations and performances that privilege a male-centric conception of racial solidarity. The ruptures that tore through the Black community were every bit as seismic as those that engulfed the society writ large, and in some ways, were perhaps more profound. Yet the media were able to capture only some dimensions of this rupture, positioned as curious onlookers seeking the occasional commentary from an inside informer. In the contemporary analysis surrounding this polarizing social event, there was little sustained commentary or analysis that parsed the intense ideological war that Anita Hill's testimony ignited within the Black community. Instead, the division was largely played as an interesting but ultimately incomprehensible wrinkle on an otherwise fully legible tale of a race versus gender contestation.

In the midst of this whiteout, a few Black women and men stepped forward to disrupt and complicate the easy erasures of the intersectional dimensions of the race and gender frames. These feminists created a grassroots campaign to buy their way into a conversation that was being conducted about them but not with them—to quickly deliver notes from the frontlines of the cultural war unfolding in their midst. This was an undertaking that was every bit as dramatic and unimaginable as the Senate invasion that spurred the Judiciary Committee into action and was in many ways more costly. Yet, the trajectory of this historical undertaking is not celebrated or remembered as "speaking truth to power." The fact that the uprising that these women—

Elsa Barkley Brown, Deborah King, Barbara Ransby and the sixteen hundred others—staged remains unmarked and largely unknown to many of those who commemorate the Anita Hill hearings is a lasting testament to the continued difficulties in incorporating more complex retellings of key events in feminist and antiracist history. It also grounds a call to resist the dominant frames that easily and predictably cast matters of race and gender into either/or narratives even as "intersectionality" gains rhetorical traction and symbolic representation. Once again the dominant frame through which the events are understood and remembered shrinks the rhetorical real estate upon which "othered" histories can deliver political meaning. In so doing, the possibilities of learning from and transcending the unfortunate fractures between gender and race politics—fractures that helped facilitate Thomas's confirmation—remain relevant today. Ironically, the multiple "failures to remember" that reinforced the unfortunate and ultimately fatal opposition between race and gender discourses in the Thomas-Hill affair remain evident today as one of the more troubling legacies of that event.

STUNNED BUT NOT BOWED

Every Black woman—and man—who took part in resisting the call to close ranks around Clarence Thomas has a moment to tell in which the painful choice between supporting Anita Hill and joining the swelling community of Thomas's supporters was made apparent. My moment came the evening following the first day of testimony. I'd come to the Capitol to support Anita Hill and together with another African American law professor, Taunya Banks, (the number of Black women law professors was small enough that most of us were at least casually acquainted with each other) we began working the phones trying to find African Americans, particularly men, to speak back against Clarence Thomas's breathtaking appropriation of the tragic history of racial terrorism. Later that evening, two African American men, Luke Charles Harris, and Carlton Long, showed up to join what they thought was the Black men's brigade and found out that they were it.

The hallways where the hearings took place was a cacophony of noise—news media were everywhere, and in front of virtually every camera, the Republican machine was amplifying the narrative that was unfolding inside: a character assault that followed an age-old pattern of stereotype and sexual innuendo against Black women. The new wrinkle here was that the performance was unfolding at the instigation of a Black man under the subscript of antiracism. Our men's brigade took to the airwaves, finding every opportunity that came our way to resist Thomas's efforts to occupy the mantle of antiracism and to remind people that Anita Hill was not telling a story that should have been a mystery to most African Americans.

After a long day of pushing back against what appeared to be an avalanche of insults, we emerged from the Capitol and found ourselves surrounded by members of the very community whose image was hanging in the balance, African American women. Encircling the venue, standing hand in hand, they lifted their voices in prayer and song, calling on God Almighty to deliver Clarence Thomas from this tribulation and to safely install his servant to the Supreme Court.[3] Shaken and disturbed, we pushed our way to what we had hoped would be the emo-

---

3. This effort was a piece of the Pin Point Strategy, a campaign initiated by the Republican Party to generate grassroots support for Clarence Thomas. The cam-

tional safe harbor of a quiet taxi, only to encounter the psychic violence of Black talk radio with angry voices hurling accusations and racist names toward the woman who we had come to DC to support. The harangue was interethnic and apparently diasporic, we noted, as our taxi driver, an African immigrant, nearly drove off the road while wildly gesticulating his conviction that this Black woman was nothing but a traitor to our community.[4] Not lost in the moment was the irony about how quickly, seemingly effortlessly, this nominee, who had committed himself to resisting the logics that underwrote this solidarity, would emerge as the exclusive beneficiary of it.

Stunned but not bowed, our experience was magnified a thousand fold as Black feminists around the country were spurred into action, angered by the way the Black community was being corralled into an undifferentiated mass in the mainstream press,

---

paign was wrapped around the theme of "Up From Georgia" and featured a bus tour of supporters who began their ride in Pin Point, Georgia, and ended at the Capitol, representing, apparently, support among the masses for the nominee. See Kimberlé Crenshaw, "Stranger than Fiction," review of *Strange Justice: The Selling of Clarence Thomas*, eds. Jane Mayer and Jill Abramson, *California Lawyer* 15 (February 1995): 63. http://www.callawyer.com/clstory.cfm?pubdt=NaN&eid=23532&evid=1. See also Jane Mayer and Jill Abramson, eds., *Strange Justice: The Selling of Clarence Thomas* (Boston: Houghton Mifflin, Harcourt, 1994), 189–91, detailing how African American organizations were funded by white conservative backers to pronounce support for Thomas's nomination.

4. See Kimberlé Crenshaw, "Whose Story Is It, Anyway? Feminist and Antiracist Appropriations of Anita Hill," in *Race-ing Justice, En-gendering Power*, ed. Toni Morrison (New York: Pantheon, 1992), 411, 420–21, stating that commentators often times were "less interested in exploring whether the allegations were true than in speculating why Hill would compromise the upward mobility of a black man and embarrass the African-American community"). See also, Michael C. Dawson, *Black Visions: The Roots of Contemporary African-American Political Ideologies* (Chicago: University of Chicago Press, 2001), 149, discussing how commentators such as Julia Hare saw Hill as a traitor and betrayer of the Black community and believed Blacks who opposed Thomas were "white-oriented, assimilationist 'coconut' feminists and their hangdog male cohorts."

and appalled by the way that Anita Hill was being pilloried in the Black press. As many critics would write in the aftermath of this debacle, race and racism were figured as the exclusive platform on which Clarence Thomas stood, squaring off against the racially unmarked figure of Anita Hill as "everywoman." In that moment there was an almost complete absence of any commentary that addressed how race and gender were figured across these supposed competing platforms. While it was Thomas who tamed the Senate and rallied the forces by waving the bloody rope, it was Anita Hill who was asphyxiated in the toxic interface of race and gender stereotypes.

The debates that circulated in the Black community and that occasionally erupted into the mainstream press served to remind us that the racial patriarchy that animated these dynamics were not by any means the exclusive preserve of the white imagination.[5] The ease by which African American sensibilities and political traditions were called into Thomas's service constituted a line in the sand for those of us who had grown tired of the patriarchal politics of racial solidarity.

An African American woman's story of workplace sexual abuse should not have been a mystery to most African Americans. After all, sexual harassment had been a staple of Black women's "employment" since their arrival to the New World. Tales of sexual abuse at the hands of employers were passed

5. See Carol J. Adams and Marie M. Fortune, eds., *Violence Against Women and Children: A Christian Theological Sourcebook* (New York: Continuum, 1995), 366, describing the variety of opinions the Black community held toward Hill, some seeing her as having been "overcome by a jealous rage and hungry for revenge" at the fact that Thomas married a white woman. But see, "Anita Hill's Detractor Apologizes for Trashing Her," ABC News, accessed June 29, 2012, http://abcnews.go.com/Politics/story?id=121534&page=1 for a discussion of how David Brock, author of *The Real Anita Hill*, admitted to having reported unverified facts, lies, and skewed conservative opinions about Hill while playing his part as a "cog in the Republican sleaze machine" to bury Hill's reputation.

down, mother to daughter, over generations, as cautionary tales about how their gender and race made them vulnerable to a special kind of workplace injury.[6] Yet the instant that Clarence Thomas denounced the hearings as nothing but "high tech lynching,"—perhaps the most brilliant rhetorical move that the now-silent justice would ever utter—everything changed. Hill's testimony became something else altogether—a white woman's thing, a complaint that conjured up images of the lying, finger-pointing "Miss Ann," whose cries of sexual violation nurtured the South's tragic crop of "Strange Fruit."[7]

Such a breathtaking erasure barely warranted comment by pundits invited to interpret this contretemps, made all the more curious by the all-Black cast of Ivy League graduates. While television commentators marveled about the group of articulate and well-poised Black lawyers in their midst, the *New York Times* turned to noted scholar Orlando Patterson for a more high-brow decoding of the sexual script at hand.[8] Patterson dutifully spun a tale that essentially excused Thomas's perjury as some sort of truth-telling by suggesting that Hill herself was the perjurer by elevating intraracial playfulness into the overheated and rigid moral terrain of white folks.[9] By this logic, Thomas may well have said all of the things that Anita Hill had described, but Hill

6. Nicole T. Buchanan and Alayne J. Ormerod, "Racialized Sexual Harassment in the Lives of African American Women," *Women and Therapy* 25 (2002): 107, 109, stating that researchers speculated that black women are reluctant to label their experiences "sexual harassment" because, ". . . in their struggle against the image of sexual promiscuity, black women may not want to draw attention to themselves as targets of sexual attention" because of their history of being labeled "sexually promiscuous, hot-blooded, and hypersexual."

7. Billie Holiday, "Strange Fruit," on *Billie Holiday*, Commodore, 1939. The "fruit" Holiday sings of signify the bodies of Black men hanging from trees in the south.

8. Orlando Patterson, "Race, Gender and Liberal Fallacies," *New York Times*, October 20, 1991, sec. 4, 15.

9. Ibid. For an expanded critique of Patterson's indictment of Hill, see Crenshaw, "Whose Story," 421–34.

was still the one who was perpetrating since she was disingenuously objecting to what was clearly recognized as a cultural style of courting. This argument amounted to a claim that Anita Hill was acting white in order to be offended by the "Rabelaisian humor" Black women supposedly hear and respond to every day.[10] Apparently, her being African American was a de facto defense to her having been harassed.

For many African American feminists, Patterson's essay was the final straw. However new and provocative the essay might have appeared to *Times* editors, the "it's just between us" defense of intraracial sexism was neither new nor convincing to thousands of women who had experienced harassment or worse at the hands of fellow African Americans. Angered that the *Times* published what was in effect an invitation to disbelieve Black women because they were "different," and that the absence of Black feminists' voices reinforced the stereotypes contained therein, many Black women clamored for a way to fight back.[11]

Refusing to be forced into scripts not of their own making, three Black feminists—Elsa Barkley Brown, Deborah King, and Barbara Ransby—penned a manifesto that captured the rage of sixteen hundred Black women.[12] Joining generations of Black women who have taken similar actions in the past, from nine-

10. Ibid, See also, Orlando Patterson, "Blacklash: The crisis of gender relations among African Americans," *Transition* 64 (1993): 7. Patterson later defended his editorial, arguing that black feminist discourse had stymied the exploration of gender relations among blacks because feminists privileged the standpoint of women due to their assumption that they were always the victims of any gender-based interaction.

11. Noting the silencing of Black women, Ransby: "In fact, it was this blatant and inexcusable exclusion of Black Womanists and feminists from the national dialogue on an issue that impinged so dramatically on our lives that inspired some of us to launch the campaign to carve out a public forum for our views—even if we had to purchase that forum with the meager resources we could collectively muster." See Barbara Ransby, "A Righteous Rage and a Grassroots Mobilization," and Elsa Barkley Brown, "Imaging Lynching," in *African American Women Speak Out*.

12. Ibid., 100.

teenth-century sisters who were forced to defend their reputations against abuse[13] to the 1970's Combahee River Collective, who spoke out against the prevailing conceptions of power that obscured the overlapping consequences of social marginality, these feminist sought to defend yet again the interests of Black women.

Their effort would be no small matter of simply speaking truth to power because in reality, without money there was no speech, no platform, no microphone that stood ready to hear what these women had to say. Silenced by the media that privileged only the "go-to" spokeswomen who were regularly quoted for "the feminist view," Black feminists were similarly overshadowed by Black male leaders who occasionally graced the mainstream airwaves and enjoyed ready access to Black media.[14] Black feminists were forced to buy their way into discourse and with the zeal of women on a mission, they began the unlikely goal of raising $50,000 to pay for an ad in the *New York Times*. In the

13. One startling example involves Black women's battles to gain access to "ladies' cars" on trains. As pointed out by Banks and Eberhardt, all women, regardless of race, were technically qualified to gain access to "ladies' cars," essentially nicer accommodations set aside for a qualified "lady," intended to be occupied by those with "good character, and genteel and modest deportment" (69). As a de facto rule, conductors would deny "[p]rostitutes and women of dubious reputation" entry as well as, quite routinely, Black women. In response to the outright denial of entry into ladies' cars, some Black women brought suit against the terms of their exclusion (ibid.). In challenging the terms of their exclusion, Black plaintiffs were faced with accusations that their "appearance" and "candor" suggested to conductors that they fell far short of the requirement of being a "lady"—in many cases plaintiffs were relentelssly questioned about their prior enslavement and their skin tone was meticulously scrutinized by judge and jury. The lighter the plaintiff's skin, the more likely courts were to determine she was a "lady" (ibid.). R. Richard Banks and Jennifer L. Eberhardt, "Social Psychological Processes and the Legal Basis of Race Categorization," in *Confronting Racism: The Problem and the Response* (Thousand Oaks, CA: SAGE, 1998).

14. Ransby noted the absence of Black feminist voices, questioning, "Where were the interviews with Barbara Smith, Audre Lorde, Mary Frances Berry, Angela Davis, Gloria Hull, June Jordan, or any of dozens of other prominent African American feminists/womanists one could name?" See Ransby, "A Righteous Rage," 45–46.

space of six weeks, Brown, King, and Ransby led an effort that assembled sixteen hundred signatures and raised the money to pay for the statement that was published November 18, 1991.[15] Entitled "African American Women in Defense of Ourselves (AAWIDOO)," the ad criticized the unproductive framing of the debacle as being either about race or about gender. Placing the treatment of Hill firmly within the history of Black women being "sexually stereotyped as immoral, insatiable, perverse," and as a consequence, "not likely to be believed," the statement declared that the interests of all Black women were at stake.[16] Importantly, the collective went on to refocus attention on what had fallen out of view in the wake of Thomas's efforts to cast the hearings as a racist plot: the entire neoconservative agenda that road with him on his way to the Supreme Court.[17] Expressing their "vehement opposition" to the agenda, the statement warned that the

15. The effort was remarkable by any standard, but even more so recognizing that this mobilization took place before the widespread use of email and online petitions to organize collectives to make political statements. See ibid., 48–50, describing the grassroots efforts that involved faxes, voicemail, snail mail, and word-of-mouth. Ransby notes as well the contributions of allies who were not Black women, including Tom Holt who contributed to the effort and who organized Black men to do the same, European American women who provided bridge loans to meet the deadlines while checks were coming in.

16. "African American Women in Defense of Ourselves," *New York Times*, November 17, 1991, advertisement, 53. Reprinted in Joy James and Tracey Denean Sharpley-Whiting, eds., *The Black Feminist Reader* (Malden, MA: Blackwell, 2000), 271, and Frances Smith Foster, Beverly Guy-Sheftall, and Stanlie M. James eds., *Still Brave: The Evolution of Black Women's Studies* (New York: The Feminist Press, 2009). The ad also appeared in several black newspapers including: the *Chicago Defender*, the [New York] *City Sun*, the *Los Angeles Sentinel*, the *San Francisco Sun Reporter*, the *D.C. Spotlight*, the *Carolinian*, and the *Atlanta Inquirer*. It was published in letter form in the *Amsterdam News*, and portions of it have been reprinted in *Essence* and *The Black Scholar*. See Ransby, "A Righteous Rage," 46.

17. See, *The Black Feminist Reader*, 272. "The Bush administration, having obstructed the passage of civil rights legislation, impeded the extension of unemployment compensation, cut student aid and dismantled social welfare programs, has continually demonstrated that it is not operating in our best interest. Nor is this appointee."

"consolidation of a conservative majority on the Supreme Court seriously endangers the rights of all women, poor and working-class people and the elderly."[18] The manifesto still stands among Black feminists as one of the most poignant moments in our own talking back, not just to the Senate, but to the Republican Party, the White House, the media, and also to the race and gender discourses that lay claim to Black women's histories while ignoring the interface between the two.

"SOMEBODY FORGOT TO TELL SOMEBODY SOMETHING"[19]

The manifesto still stands as a hint of what should have been a powerful, intersectional coalition to defeat the consolidation of an anti-civil rights, neoconservative agenda on the Supreme Court.[20] AAWIDOO's legacy is in calling to fore the reproduction of an African American politics that is male-centric, and a discourse on sexual harassment that has been underwritten by a "universal" subject that defaults to white. The entrenched pat-

18. Ibid.

19. Toni Morrison interviewed by Ntozake Shange on *It's Magic*, WBAI radio show, New York, 1978, quoted in Barbara Christian, "Somebody Forgot to Tell Somebody Something: African-American Women's Historical Novels" in Joanne M. Braxton and Andree Nicola McLaughlin, eds., *Wild Women in the Whirlwind: Afra-American Culture and the Contemporary Literary Renaissance* (New Brunswick, NJ: Rutgers University Press, 1990).

20. Nina Totenberg, "Clarence Thomas Influence On The Supreme Court" All Things Considered, NPR, http://www.npr.org/2011/10/11/141246695/clarence-thomas-influence-on-the-court, accessed June 29, 2012. Discusses how Thomas's extreme conservative positioning on many issues has made the other justices' views appear more centrist and "that by just staking out a previously inconceivable position, Thomas, even though alone, makes that position plausible." For excerpts of Justice Thomas highly conservative opinions on civil rights, such as fervently opposing affirmative action programs, see "Clarence Thomas on Civil Rights," *On The Issues*, accessed June 29, 2012. http://www.ontheissues.org/Court/Clarence_Thomas_Civil_Rights.htm

terns of political thought that these frames reproduced facilitated the ease by which Hill was disowned by many, and the difficulties many feminists faced in advancing an effective response.[21] The sexual abuse of Black women—indeed, their own experience of lynching—was completely obscured in the interpretive templates of many African Americans. The racial origins of sexual harassment were buried as well, leaving many of Hill's defenders flatfooted in the face of claims that sexual harassment was a preoccupation of white, middle-class women. Both of these liabilities were the products of historical erasures—failures to uplift and remember how Black women's political agency in addressing the interface of race and gender dominance constituted foundational elements of both the civil rights movement and the mobilization against sexual harassment.

The erasures that narrowed the interpretive terrain were buoyed in part through the uni-dimensional ways that understandings of and contestations against social power have been historicized and retold. The very same dynamics that were unfolding in the Hill-Thomas moment—the conflation of intersectional vulnerabilities into singular and opposing frames— were built upon earlier elisions that obscured the common origins of both. For example, the received narratives of the civil rights movement have been framed largely in terms of spontaneous emergence of charismatic male leadership rising up to challenge the debilitating consequences of white supremacy, most dramatically symbolized by a sexualized racism that underwrote both segregation and extralegal violence. The narrative highlights male leadership and male victimization, relegating Black women and issues that

21. A typical response among feminists was to deny the claim that race had anything to do with the matter. See for example, Eleanor Holmes Norton: "This is about sex and not about race. A black woman raised these questions, not a white woman or white men." Barkley Brown, "Imaging Lynching," 101.

shaped their political activism to secondary importance. Misremembered in this narrative has been Black women's leadership, in particular, their historical struggles against sexual racism and their understanding that their gendered experience was as central to the interests of the Black community as the victimization of men.

Black women's agency is sometimes remembered in the role as "mothers" of the movement, as in the iconography developed around Rosa Parks. In the classic telling, Parks was simply a seamstress too tired to give her seat to a white man.[22] Of course, it was known at the time that she was a seasoned activist, but the representation of Parks as a tired seamstress was both a more legible and palatable image to foreground.[23] Only with the more nuanced telling of Parks's activist history is the full scope of Parks's political trajectory revealed. Rosa Parks's first act of courage was not refusing to give up her seat on that Montgomery bus,[24] but her refusal to accept the likely acquittal of a gang of white men who raped a Black woman many years earlier in 1944.[25] Parks stood up against the routine denigration of Black women in a manner that was far more life threatening

22. See, "The Road to Civil Rights: Too Tired to Move," Highway History, US Department of Transportation, Federal Highway Administration, accessed July 2, 2012. http://www.fhwa.dot.gov/highwayhistory/road/s23.cfm. Tellingly, the description of the event posted on a federal department's website makes no mention of Parks's depth of involvement in the wider civil rights movement.

23. See Adam Fairclough, *To Redeem the Soul of America: The Southern Christian Leadership Conference and Martin Luther King, Jr,* (Atlanta, GA: University of Georgia Press, 2001), 16, noting Parks's history in dealing with segregation, such as her long membership with the NAACP and her participation and training at the interracial Highlander Folk School.

24. See Danielle L. McGuire, *At the Dark End of the Street: Black Women, Rape, and Resistance—A New History of the Civil Rights Movement from Rosa Parks to the Rise of Black Power* (New York: Vintage, 2010).

25. Ibid., 13, detailing Parks's efforts in building a legal strategy for attaining justice for the rape victim, Recy Taylor.

than her role in galvanizing the Montgomery bus boycott. Parks and other African American women who took up the dangerous work of defending Black women against sexual terrorism recognized the inextricable dimensions of white supremacy and sexual violence,[26] blending womanist consciousness together with antiracism at the very foundation of the civil rights movement. Resistance to sexual violence was thus far from a post-movement afterthought or a white feminist spin-off. Unearthing Parks and other Black women's activism over time reveals that the gendered dimensions of racial exploitation experienced by Black women were not alien to but fully constitutive of the way that racism was understood. Yet this memory has not been nurtured and retold but buried beneath shame and ambivalence. Its consequence in the Hill-Thomas affair was a male-centered frame on sexual racism that anointed Clarence Thomas as a victim and left Anita Hill outside the politics of empathy and group recognition. As a consequence of this forgetting to tell, the singular trope of lynching served as both shield and sword, to deflect the charges against Thomas, and to forcibly separate Hill and her supporters from Black communal politics.

At the same time that this distorted vision of antiracism failed the task of capturing what was happening to Anita Hill, the era-

26. Often relegated to the background, Black women built and sustained the infrastructure of the civil rights movement, a fact dramatically illustrated by the Montgomery Bus Boycott. See Jo Ann Gibson Robinson and David J. Garrow, *The Montgomery Bus Boycott and the Women Who Started It: The Memoir of Jo Ann Gibson Robinson* (Knoxville, TN: University of Tennessee Press, 1987); Vicki L. Crawford, Jacqueline Ann Rouse, and Barbara Woods, eds., *Women in the Civil Rights Movement: Trailblazers and Torchbearers, 1941–1965* (Bloomington, IN: Indiana University Press, 1993); Belinda Robnett, "African-American Women in the Civil Rights Movement, 1954–1965: Gender, Leadership, and Micromobilization," *American Journal of Sociology* 101, (1996): 1661; Bettye Collier-Thomas and Vincent P. Franklin, eds., *Sisters in the Struggle: African American Women in the Civil Rights-Black Power Movement* (New York: New York University Press, 2001).

sure of Black women's foundational role in establishing sexual harassment contributed to a perception that sexual harassment was incompatible with African American interests and sensibilities.[27] Hill's defenders were sometimes left with only an assertion of the essential racelessness in this form of gender discrimination in the face of claims that harassment was a white woman's preoccupation. The critique carried additional sting within Black politics given longstanding suspicions that many lynchings began as consensual affairs between Black men and white women who later participated in the deadly denunciation.[28] Sexual harassment became a newer version of an old narrative, extending Black men's vulnerability not only to the workplace but to the reckless finger pointing of Black women themselves. By this measure, Anita Hill was placed in the lineage of white women's

27. See Patterson, "Race, Gender and Liberal Fallacies," arguing that Black people's "down home courting" style was culturally distinct from whites and that Hill was acting disingenuously in feigning offense; Lynn Norment, "Black Men, Black Women and Sexual Harassment," *Ebony* magazine, January 1992, 118. Sociologist Robert Staples is quoted as saying "[t]here are cultural differences in how Black men approach Black women, and if that is taken onto a job, then one would not expect Black women to be offended by it, unless it was asked in exchange for a job or promotion"). Aside from the troubling inference that Black women who take offense at behavior that Staples would claim as "culturally distinct" should be disregarded as cultural outliers, this argument simply reproduces that basic failure to understand harassment in terms that transcend quid pro quo offenses. See note 2 and Kimberlé Crenshaw, "Race, Gender, and Sexual Harassment," *Southern California Law Review* 65 (1991); 1467, 1471–72, discussing how feminists helped maintain the prevailing narrative structures, which lacked an intersectional perspective, and thus directly advantaged Thomas's position to claim that he was the victim of racial discrimination with Hill as the perpetrator, by framing the Anita Hill event as being either a race or a gender issue. See also, Catharine A. MacKinnon, "From Practice to Theory, or What Is A White Woman Anyway?," *Yale Journal of Law and Feminism* 4 (1991): 13, 17–18, recounting the stories of two Black women, Mechelle Vinson and Lillian Garland, whose lawsuits against sexual harassment and sexual discrimination, respectively, helped pave the way for all women on these issues.

28. See, Paula J. Giddings, *Ida: A Sword Among Lions: Ida B. Wells and the Campaign Against Lynching* (New York: Harper Collins, 2009), 221, discussing how revealing the truth behind the consensual nature of many of these interactions

false accusations, further reifying the race versus gender frame that the media was pounding on a day-to-day basis.

This narrative also was a product of forgetting, specifically, the fact that it was Black women who were the plaintiffs in the landmark cases that established sexual harassment as workplace discrimination.[29] Interrogating the sociopolitical dynamics that were at play in the aftermath of the civil rights movement, the links between the interpersonal revolution that the civil rights movement spawned and its embodiment by Black women in resisting their longstanding vulnerabilities to sexual abuse might be fruitfully recovered. The African American freedom movement embodied a stance toward racial power that had public as well as private dimensions. The efforts to politicize the personal as well as the institutional aspects of white supremacy were perhaps best captured through insistent demands for interpersonal respect. Perhaps the most meaningful example of this demand is the remarkably successful embargo of the use of "boy" and other nomenclature that signaled the second-class status of African American men. The fact that these signals of racialized power were so thoroughly linked to intolerable conditions of the past

---

between Black men and white women would challenge the view of "bestiality" of Black men, and "the necessity to chivalrously defend the purity of pure white womanhood against blacks of all classes." See also, Mia Bay, *To Tell the Truth Freely: The Life of Ida B. Wells* (New York: Hill and Wang, 2009), 102, describing how Wells would investigate, interview members of the community where a lynching occurred, and discover that consensual relations between Black men and white women were often times at the heart of fabricated rapes allegations.

29. See Meritor Sav. Bank v. Vinson, 477 US 57 (1986) establishing that sexual harassment in a working environment, such as a woman being raped by ones employer and him waving his penis and laughing at her, is sex discrimination under civil rights law. See also, California Fed. Sav. & Loan Ass'n v. Guerra. 479 US 272 (1987) establishing that guaranteeing unpaid leave for pregnant women by law is not discrimination on the basis of sex.

no matter who it was who uttered the words is demonstrated by the fact that even the intraracial use of the term can be read as a racial sign of disrespect. For Black women, the interpersonal dimensions of racial power that they faced would include their vulnerability as targets of sexual abuse. And like the discourses pertaining to Black men, the intraracial reproduction of these patterns of abuse do not place them outside the realm of racial power. In the same way that Black women have learned that white men can and do treat Black women differently, the license to treat Black women differently from white women may also be understood as racial even when it is Black men who take such liberties. That these behaviors are framed as "cultural" may simply point to the ubiquity of the practices themselves, or equally, the lack of any serious threat of sanction for intraracial sexual abuse.

For a generation of Black women who lived through and were shaped by the dramatic interpersonal transformations of the freedom movement, the understandings associated with personal integrity and respect may have contributed to Black women's ability to understand sexual harassment through the lens of racial disempowerment. Understanding the experiences through this frame would not only encourage the belief that suffering these insults in private was no longer tolerable, but further, that resistance to unwanted sexual encounters was a legitimate expression of the demand for racial equality. If being called "boy" was a political act that warranted resistance and censure, how could it be that being expected to endure treatment that was long associated with Black women's sexual vulnerability was not equally intolerable? When interpreted through this lens, harassing behavior was less likely to be understood as a misplaced effort to date or boorish expressions of passion or

harassment. In matters of women and political leadership, the involvement of women in politics has remained a focal point of activism. Much of this sentiment was marshaled in Hillary Clinton's bid for the White House and perhaps is more profoundly demonstrated in the dramatic growth of women in the ranks of Republican representatives.[31] I present neither of these features as unmitigated successes, but only to mark the extent to which the terms upon which the "Boxer rebellion" was understood have continued to resonate as interventions against the conditions that still exist. But the question of AAWIDOO's legacy is more complicated. Has this intervention been institutionalized and amplified in practice? Can it be said that there is no longer a need for Black women to buy our way into public space, even in public discourses explicitly about the Black community? Can we rest comfortably in the recognition that a costly opposition between feminism and antiracism will never happen again?

An assessment of AAWIDOO's legacy should be taken up more systematically and more rigorously than this context can permit, but at least some well-known developments would suggest considerably less traction than the more mainstream rebellion has garnered. In the years following Thomas's confirmation there were numerous events that seemed to reinforce the poli-

31. Growing from thirty-three Republican women in the 102nd Congress (1991–1993), to ninety-two in the 112th (2011–2013). See, Jennifer Manning and Colleen Shogan, *Women in the United States Congress: 1917–2011* (Washington, DC: Congressional Research Service, 2011).

tics that AAWIDOO rallied against. In 1995 Minister Louis Farakkhan rallied African American men to participate in the Million Man March, a march on Washington that was notable for disinviting over half of the constituency that made up the African American community: Black women.[32] Marginalizing once again Black feminist voices, the media's coverage focused almost exclusively on allegations of anti-Semitism while the glaring misogyny that typified much of the minister's discourse on women remained completely uninterrogated.[33] Once again, Black feminists had to force their way into the debate by staging their own press conference to protest the exclusionary protest.

We know further the failed lessons offered by AAWIDOO in the controversy over Mike Tyson when African American leaders planned a hero's welcome upon his release from prison after having been convicted of raping Desiree Washington. Once again, the gendered politics of racial solidarity was revealed in the parade that celebrated his homecoming and by the taunts of treachery that were thrown at the many Black women who opposed him.[34]

32. Minister Louis Farrakhan requested "a million sober, disciplined, committed, dedicated, inspired black men to meet in Washington on a day of atonement," and the exclusion of women from the march ironically was meant to signify a move toward unity. See, Charles Bierbauer, "Its goal more widely accepted than its leader," *CNN*, October 17, 1995, http://www-cgi.cnn.com/US/9510/megamarch/10-17/notebook/.

33. See Marlene Cimons, "'Unity' March Exclusion Divides Women: Washington: Some Attend Event Anyway to Bring Their Sons or Simply to Show Solidarity. But Others, Including Angela Davis, Criticize Sexism," *Los Angeles Times*, October 17, 1995, quoting Angela Davis as saying, "No march, movement or agenda that defines manhood in the narrowest terms and seeks to make women lesser partners in this quest for equality can be considered a positive step. . . . There are ways of understanding black masculinity that do not rely on subjugating women."

34. See, Kimberlé Crenshaw, "Mapping the Margins: Intersectionality, Identity Politics, and Violence Against Women of Color," *Stanford Law Review* 43 (1991):

AAWIDOO's lost lessons are evident in a host of other insults that, like the Thomas event, are slung at Black women, foe and friend alike. AAWIDOO's lost lessons are apparent when Black women are still cast as the nappy headed ho's in the Imus debacle,[35] or as the charicature of Shirley Sherrod, cast as a simple-minded reverse racist that the NAACP called for the White House to summarily terminate her without as much as a phone call.[36]

When we are the irresponsible defaulters in the subprime scandal,[37] the illegitimate stay-at-home moms in the welfare

---

1241, 1273, revealing how Black leaders such as Benjamin Hooks and Louis Far-rakhan made their support of Tyson known, while no significant Black voice came to the defense of Washington. See also, Wiley A. Hall, "Mike Tyson Returns to Cheers and Jeers," *Baltimore Sun*, June 22, 1995, describing Tyson's return to Harlem after his three-year stint in jail as being met with celebration featuring the likes of Rev. Al Sharpton, Hooks, and the support of fifty-two Harlem area churches.

35. See, Russell K. Robinson, "Racing the Closet," *Stanford Law Review* 61 (2009): 1463, 1507, discussing how an artist extended Imus's "nappy headed ho's" insult to the daughters of President Obama. See also David Carr, "Networks Condemn Remarks by Imus," *New York Times*, April 7, 2007, B7; Bill Carter and Jacques Steinberg, "Off the Air: The Light Goes Out for Don Imus," *New York Times*, April 13, 2007, C1.

36. See, "Fox News' Long History of Race-Baiting," *Media Matters*, June 13, 2011, http://mediamatters.org/research/201106130023, for an examination of how Sherrod was just one in a long line of victims of Fox's reverse-racism ideology, and Stephanie Condon, "Are Liberals Too Concerned With Being 'Colorblind'?," CBS News, July 22, 2010, noting that liberals' concern with colorblindness has resulted in them "ceding the debate to the right" and, in Sherrod's case, has resulted in reactive pandering in isolated incidents. See also, Earl Ofari Hutchinson, "NAACP Still Hasn't Atoned for Sherrod Blunder," *The Huffington Post*, July 14, 2010, http://www.huffingtonpost.com/earl-ofari-hutchinson/naacp-still-hasnt-atoned_b_658120.html, detailing how the NAACP failed to issue a call to the agriculture department for Sherrod's reinstatement, or call for an apology to Sherrod, or demand that the altered video at the core of the controversy be taken down, displaying the NAACP's failure to properly take responsibility for its actions and harm to Sherrod.

37. "ACORN's Aim: Chaos at the Polls," *RushLimbaugh.com*, October 14, 2008, http://img.rushlimbaugh.com/home/daily/site_101408/content/01125113.guest.html, blaming the US Government's welfare policies for the prevalence of single

debate,[38] the producers of the badly parented miscreants in the crime reports every day,[39] the mules,[40] the enablers, the co-conspirators who make up the fastest growing casualties in America's endless war on drugs[41] and in the wake of the Diallo-Strauss-Kahn controversy, we are the manipulative, money-hungry, rape accuser, the "real" villain who operates behind the facade of the hard-working immigrant, the woman who steals

Black women households, and arguing that these same policies played a deep role in the subprime mortgage crisis. See also, Andrea Harris, "Unsustainable Loans, in The National Urban League," in *The State of Black America 2008: In The Black Woman's Voice*, The National Urban League Report, 2008, 125, 126, indicating that Black women were five times more likely than white men to receive subprime loans in 2006. See also, Ovetta Wiggins, "Suffering in Silence Over Foreclosure In Upscale Subdivision, Few Know the Troubles Neighbors Face," *Washington Post*, March 16, 2008, sec. A, discussing how a predominately Black neighborhood, even a very upscale one, experienced the foreclosure crises in a manner indicative of the national trend, which showed the amount of subprime loans received by Black families as much more common than by white families.

38. Cristina Gallo, "Marrying Poor: Women's Citizenship, Race, and Tanf Policies," *UCLA Women's Law Journal* 19 (2012): 61, 88, discussing the anti-Black racist and sexist attack on Black women portrayed as "welfare queen" by antagonists of the welfare system, even though the absolute share of recipients of welfare who were Black women decreased from the 60s to the 90s.

39. Catherine R. Albiston and Laura Beth Nielsen, "Welfare Queens and Other Fairy Tales: Welfare Reform and Unconstitutional Reproductive Controls," *Howard Law Journal* 38 (1995): 473, 482. "To justify denying social welfare benefits to Black women, policy makers argued that Black deviant 'culture' was inherited and that 'the baby was likely to be as great a social liability as its mother.'"

40. See, Anderson v. Cornejo, 355 F.3d 1021, 1024–25 (7th Cir. 2004) where a group of ninety Black women who brought suit against the United States Customs Service for having been subjected to non-routine searches, such as x-rays and strip searches, and found to have not been carrying any contraband, were denied judgment despite statistics showing that Black women were nine times more likely to be stopped than white women, because 27.6 percent of stops still resulted in finding contraband. If anything, the court argued, "Customs officials are conducting too few searches, not too many."

41. Brittney Mazza, "Women and Prison Industrial Complex: The Criminalization of Gender, Race and Class in the 'War on Drugs,'" *Dialogues@RU Journal* 5 (2006): 79, 81–82, http://dialogues.rutgers.edu/about-the-journal/student-research-papers/

our resources, compromises our good will, and embarrasses us on the world stage.[42]

Yes, Black women still find themselves defending their name, often alone, almost always against foes, sometimes against friends. But the constant demand to defend our name is only one of the continuities from the Hill-Thomas event. Equally troubling is the trajectory of Thomas's strategy of mobilizing a male-centered antiracism to serve right-wing ends. Its many consequences can be seen today in the belief, for example, that targeted intervention to Black men and boys will simply trickle down to Black women and girls, a view that ignores the structural and institutional dimension of inequality across gender, race, and class.[43] But the real dividend here has been the elevation of family formation and individualism as the real source of inequality, squashing structural remedies and facilitating redistribution of wealth upward.[44] The eclipse of broader, structural remedies

---

cat_view/12-volume-v. "The 'war on drugs' is often claimed to be waged in defense of public safety and family values; however, it often results in much more harm than good for the African American community and family, with particularly devastating consequences for minority females."

42. See "No Longer Welcome," *New York Post*, August 24, 2011, http://www.nypost.com/p/news/opinion/editorials/no_longer_welcome_t7suy3KUG6mLTPqf-FazVeI, illustrating the opinion held by commentators that Diallo was a fraud, and should be deported for her actions.

43. See, Kimberlé W. Crenshaw, "Close Encounters of Three Kinds: On Teaching Dominance Feminism and Intersectionality," *Tulsa Law Review* 46 (2010): 151, 185–87. See also, Ayanna Brown, "Descendants of 'Ruth:' Black Girls Coping Through the 'Black Male Crisis,'" *The Urban Review* 43 (2011): 597, 600. "The emphasis on the condition and opportunities for Black males has helped to construct a unitary framework for oppression. Consequently, Black girls are treated as a variable within these discussions, or Black girls are otherwise pitted-against Black boys. Therefore, frameworks that stratify Black men and Black women reinforce a dominant cultural view for gender roles".

44. Thomas Kleven, "Systemic Classism, Systemic Racism: Are Social and Racial Justice Achievable in the United States?," *Connecticut Public Interest Law Journal* 8 (2009): 37, 68.

for racial inequality has been eased by the limiting focus on Black male endangerment, most often framed as correctable only through sustained programs to encourage male responsibility. These programs seldom engage institutional and structural dimensions of racial inequality, and rarely if ever address the specific needs and challenges facing Black women and girls. The widespread institutional focus on Black men and boys as framed through the "endangerment" context has left Black women to fend for themselves.

AAWIDOO is still relevant today, not simply as a defense of Black women, but as a vision of social justice advocacy that draws attention to the unfortunate erasures that create the opportunity for racial retrenchment.

I want to end by telling you that I still have my "I Believe Anita Hill" t-shirt and a yellowed copy of the *New York Times* ad hangs on the wall of our family home where my mother, a proud signatory of that statement, hung it some twenty years ago. Both of these artifacts serve as reminders to me not to forget to tell somebody about the many rebellions that were set in motion by Hill's testimony. And I want to say that I think we need to talk and think about what's next, what needs to be marked here and now, what needs to be memorialized, organized and projected through the culture, through our networks, through our politics.

KIMBERLE WILLIAMS CRENSHAW, professor of law at UCLA and Columbia Law School, is a leading authority in the area of civil rights, Black feminist legal theory, and race, racism, and the law. She is the founding coordinator of the Critical Race Theory Workshop, and the co-editor of *Critical Race Theory: Key Documents That Shaped the Movement*. Crenshaw has facilitated workshops for human rights activists in Brazil and

India, and for constitutional court judges in South Africa. Her ground-breaking work on intersectionality was influential in the drafting of the equality clause in the South African Constitution. In 1996, she co-founded the African American Policy Forum to house a variety of projects designed to deliver research-based strategies to better advance social inclusion. Twice awarded Professor of the Year at UCLA Law School, Crenshaw received the Lucy Terry Prince Unsung Heroine Award presented by the Lawyers' Committee on Civil Rights Under Law, and the Founders Award from the Coalition of 100 Black Women. Crenshaw has received the ACLU Ira Glasser Racial Justice Fellowship, the Fulbright Distinguished Chair for Latin America, and the Alphonse Fletcher Fellowship. Currently, Crenshaw is the faculty director of the Center for Intersectionalilty and Social Policy Studies at Columbia Law School.

SEX, POWER, AND CHANGE: WHERE DO WE GO NOW?

VIRGINIA VALIAN

O n October 9, 1991, the *New York Times* and CBS polled 512 adults about their impressions of Anita Hill and Clarence Thomas.[1] The poll took place after Hill's testimony of Thomas's sexual harassment but before all the testimony concerning Thomas's alleged harassment had been presented. A majority of people were either undecided or did not believe Hill: 47 percent of people thought that Hill's charges were probably false, 32 percent were undecided, and only 21 percent thought they were probably true. Although a minority of people—23 percent— thought that Thomas should be confirmed if the charges against him were true, a majority—56 percent—thought that he should be confirmed if there was doubt about whether the charges were true. Since most people either thought the charges were not true or were undecided, they gave Thomas the benefit of the doubt. Seventy five percent of the people polled also thought that the Senate Judiciary Committee had treated Professor Hill fairly.

The "people" then had about the same views as the sena-

1. The adults had previously been interviewed about a month earlier, on the eve of the hearings to determine whether Thomas should be confirmed.

tors who confirmed Thomas. Of the fifty-two who voted to confirm him, eleven were Democrats, most of them from southern states, and the rest were Republicans. Of the forty-eight who voted against confirmation, only two were Republicans and one of them later changed his affiliation.[2]

In that same 1991 *New York Times* poll, almost 40 percent of the women surveyed said that they had been the object of sexual advances, or a proposition, or unwanted sexual discussions from men who supervised them or who could affect their position at work. Ninety percent of the women in that poll who said that they had experienced some form of sexual harassment also said that they did not report it.

Then and subsequently, not reporting harassment has been the norm. A study by the US Merit Systems Protection Board, published in 1995, had several major findings concerning "unwanted sexual attention" in the federal workplace.

First, the survey showed reasonable understanding on the part of both men and women in the US of what constituted sexual harassment, an understanding aided by training and perhaps also by the Hill-Thomas hearings. The legal definition is (perhaps surprisingly) broad: unwelcome sexual advances, requests for sexual favors, and other verbal or physical conduct of a sexual nature constitute sexual harassment when submission to such conduct is made either explicitly or implicitly a term or condition of an individual's employment, submission to or rejection of such conduct by an individual is used as the basis for employment decisions affecting such individuals, or such conduct has the purpose or effect of unreasonably interfering with an individual's work performance or creating an intimidating, hostile,

2. Calculated by the author from US Senate records.

or offensive working environment. Sexual harassment as legally defined is thus somewhat different from gender harassment, which is sexual and sexist hostility that suggests that the person's gender inherently prevents them from doing their job at a competent level or should count as a reason for them not to have the job, regardless of their competence.

A second finding was that milder forms of harassment, which include unwanted sexual teasing, jokes, remarks, or questions, are the most common types. Third, rates of harassment were very similar between 1987 and 1994, and higher for female than male victims, averaging 43 percent for women and 16 percent for men. Fourth, very few individuals—6 percent—ever formally reported their harasser; about half the victims thought that their experience wasn't serious enough for a formal report. Informal responses, such as telling the harasser to stop, were more frequent, but 44 percent of victims did nothing at all. Fifth, most individuals who experienced harassment—78 percent—mentioned co-workers, but 28 percent of women and 14 percent of men mentioned supervisors.

In sum, even at the time of the hearings in 1991, there were data available to show how common harassment was in the federal workplace and how seldom it was reported. The main reason people were skeptical of Hill's allegations was that she had not reported Thomas's behavior at the time. Yet her behavior was—and remains—normative. Most people who experience harassment discuss the issue with a friend or coworker, but very few people report it and even fewer bring the alleged offender to court (e.g., Fitzgerald, Swan, and Fischer, 1995). Women fear not being believed, being humiliated, or being retaliated against, and losing their possibility of advancement (Fitzgerald, Swan and Fischer, 1995). Although it seems scarcely necessary to say so, harassment—sexual, racial, or both—has negative consequences for the individuals who experience it (e.g., Buchanan and Fitzgerald, 2008; Willness, Steel, and Lee, 2007).

A subsequent analysis of the government's 1994 data found that harassment was greatest for women between the ages of twenty-five and forty-four (Anita Hill's age at the time of the alleged harassment), and greater for women with more education and for women at higher pay grades (Newman, Jackson, and Baker, 2003).

We have learned a lot about harassment since 1991—about how frequently it occurs, about who the victims are, about who the harassers are, and about the workplaces where it is most common (Gutek, 2001). Sexual harassment affects women more than men, but estimates vary widely; in some studies, men report harassment at levels close to women.[3] Sex also interacts with ethnicity. A phone survey conducted in 2003–2004 found that women reported sexual harassment at rates greater than men between the ages of thirty-one and sixty (Rospenda, Richman, and Shannon, 2009). When stratified by education, significant differences between men and women were only found for those with college or graduate degrees, though the same pattern was found at lower levels of education.[4] Among whites, women reported significantly more harassment than men did (51 per-

3. Gutek (1985) suggests that men may be more likely than women to label expressions of sexual interest on the part of a co-worker as harassment, while women may be more likely than men to reserve the term for unwelcome advances. In addition, men tend to be harassers: most harassers of women are men, and half the harassers of men are other men.

4. Differences as a function of education are as likely to reflect understanding of what constitutes sexual harassment as to reflect differences in experiences. In one study, blue-collar women did not interpret an employer's asking for sex as a condition of advancement to be sexual harassment (Icenogle, Eagle, Ahmad, and Hanks, 2002).

cent of women versus 39 percent of men), but among blacks the trend was reversed because of the very high rates reported by men (53 percent of women versus 69 percent of men). Unmarried women and men experience more harassment than those who are married.

We also know that although harassment of women can occur in all types of organizations, it is more likely to occur in organizations that have inadequate complaint procedures and that have a small percentage of women, especially a small percentage of women in positions of power, for example, firefighters and police officers (see reviews by O'Leary-Kelly, Bowes-Sperry, Bates, and Lean, 2009; McDonald, 2012, Willness, et al, 2007). Although anyone can harass, we know that men are much more likely to be harassers than women. Over 90 percent of harassers of women are men and about 40 to 50 percent of harassers of men are men.

We know some of the characteristics of men who harass women (see, e.g., O'Leary-Kelly et al, 2009). They implicitly perceive a close relation between sex and power. Women are not harassed because they are attractive. Rather, men who harass women see them as attractive because of existing power differentials or because of a desire to create a power difference. If, in addition, such men are unlikely to suffer any consequences due to their harassment, they will continue.

At the time of Thomas's confirmation hearings, I tried desperately and unsuccessfully to get a senator to talk to experts on sexual harassment and to have those experts testify. But expert testimony was exactly the information that then Senator Joseph Biden, chair of the Senate Judiciary Committee, decided should *not* be presented. Information about how harassment works and the normative response to harassment, both of which were present in Hill's testimony, was information that the Senate and the

American people needed to hear. But Biden decided that no context would be permitted, in effect requiring people to make their judgments from a position of profound ignorance.

We have made strides in education, but we need to do more to educate lawyers, lawmakers, judges, and Supreme Court justices. We need to ensure that everyone understands how gender works and the conditions that give rise to biased decision-making. From cognitive psychology we know that fast decisions tend to rely on stereotypes, rather than a full examination of the evidence. If, in addition, decision makers are prevented from having the evidence, good decisions will be in short supply.

Sexual harassment is an egregious abuse of power in the workplace. But there are many more subtle instances where those without power, for example, women and people of color, are disadvantaged. These instances are omnipresent but subtle. They tend not to be recognized, even though they culminate in the paucity of women and people of color in positions of status and achievement. Research on workplace incivility, or types of harassment that are not overtly sexual or gendered, suggest that women are more likely than men to be the targets (Cortina, Magley, Williams, and Langhout, 2001). And women who experience sexual harassment are also likely to experience workplace incivility; the behaviors tend to be correlated (Lim and Cortina, 2005).

In *Why So Slow? The Advancement of Women*, I discuss the reasons underlying the paucity of women and people of color in positions of status and prestige in situations that seem benign and meritocratic. There are two interlocking processes—the operation of gender schemas and the accumulation of advantage. Gender schemas are (largely nonconscious) beliefs that both men and women share about the characteristics of men and women. Because we see men as more competent than women, we slightly overvalue their contributions in many small ways. Those small examples accumulate to benefit men in professional settings.

What we know about gender in the workplace can be illustrated with a small example: the meeting. At the meeting a woman makes a comment and everyone ignores it. Ten minutes later, Joe, to pick a name at random, makes the same comment and everybody says, "Joe, what a great idea!" This common occurrence—in which a woman is ignored and a man is attended to—is one that people generally do not know how to handle, even if they notice it. It doesn't even qualify as workplace incivility. If the person who is ignored says something about it to one of her well-intentioned colleagues, she's likely to be told, "Don't make a mountain out of a molehill." Or, "Don't sweat the small stuff." Or, "Concentrate on the things that really matter."

That is where the idea of the accumulation of advantage comes in. People become successful by parlaying small gains into bigger gains. If you do not get your fair share of those small gains, such as by being listened to in a meeting or by having your accomplishments recognized, then you do not have the opportunity to make large gains. Mountains *are* molehills, piled one on top of the other. Each of those molehills matters. Over time they accumulate to give women a disadvantage (Martell, Lane, and Emrich, 1996). Men, in effect, get more interest on their achievements than women do. Both men and women are likely to underrate a woman's performance in a task that requires competence. Both women and men are likely to see a woman who is successful as less likeable than a male who is successful (Heilman, Wallen, Fuchs, and Tamkins, 2004). Both women and men are likely to sabotage the behavior of a woman who succeeds at a counter-stereotypic task, a task that we would associate with men (Rudman, Moss-Racusin, Phelan, and Nauts, 2011; Rudman and Phelan, 2008).

We need the idea of gender schemas to understand why even well-intentioned people, people who are unlikely to engage in sexual or gender harassment, nevertheless treat men and women differently in the workplace, with the result that it is easier for men than for women to succeed. We need to see the connection among gender schemas, unintended differences in treatment, workplace incivility, gender harassment, and sexual harassment. They are *not* all the same, but they overlap.

Men are particularly the aggressors in sexual harassment, but in the everyday events that advantage men and disadvantage women, both men and women slightly overrate men and slightly underrate women, resulting in further and further disparities. Those disparities are revealed in everything from salary differences to rank differences. Sexual and gender harassment can be devastating, but the everyday disadvantages experienced by many more women on a daily basis also matter.

The most recent failure of the judiciary to understand how gender operates at work was the Supreme Court decision in January 2011 not to allow a class action suit brought by women against Wal-Mart Stores, Inc. to go forward. The Court held that the women who were suing did not constitute a class because they could not demonstrate a policy of discrimination. Just as lawmakers in 1991 did not understand the sexual harassment of women and women's reactions to it, lawmakers and the judiciary today do not understand how women are disadvantaged in the workplace. In particular, they do not understand that employers can have good intentions (which is not to say that Wal-Mart has good intentions), yet still systematically create situations in which it is harder for women and people of color to advance compared to white men. A stated policy against discrimination is insufficient to prevent frequent, if uncoordinated, actions that disadvantage women. Cognitive psychologists have conducted scores of experiments that demonstrate that people with the best intentions, including women, perceive women to be less competent than men. Our good intentions, our genuine belief that only merit matters, buffer us from seeing the effects of our behaviors.

WHAT CAN WE DO? TWO PRESCRIPTIONS

First, we need to be much smarter than we have been about how to influence people in power so that they will make intelligent and well-reasoned decisions. We need to be smarter about how to put people who are likely to make those intelligent and well-reasoned decisions into positions of power. We need to be much smarter about how to affect people's attitudes and behaviors. There are already many efforts to educate the judiciary, lawyers, and lawmakers, but we need to be much more systematic and determined in our efforts. We need to find the levers that will work.

The second prescription is to form rapid response teams that would provide well-documented, unbiased, and accurate information to the media as soon as the information is needed. Journalists and investigative reports want to be accurate, but they have neither the luxury of time nor the background in the relevant science. Whether the issue is insults against women by public figures or suggestions that women choose not to be successful professionals, we can put the events and data in context and explain their origins. The university setting is a natural place for such teams. We have students, faculty, and volunteers who can perform the research. At critical historical moments, like the Thomas confirmation hearings, we want to be sure that the information is widely accessible. The media have the power to spread information broadly. We need to make sure that they come to us for that information.

VIRGINIA VALIAN is a distinguished professor of psychology, linguistics, and speech language-hearing sciences at Hunter College and the Graduate Center of the City University of New York (CUNY). Valian is a cognitive scientist who works in two areas, language acquisition and gender equity. Her book, *Why So Slow? The Advancement of Women* provides a science-based explanation for the paucity of women in positions of high status. Valian is co-founder and co-director of the Hunter College Gender Equity Project, which is dedicated to advancing women in the professions, through research, education, and action. Tutorials can be accessed at www.hunter.cuny.edu/gendertutorial and resource material can be accessed at www.hunter.cuny.edu/genderequity.

WORKS CITED

Buchanan, NiCole T. and Fitzgerald, Louise F. 2008. "Effects of racial and sexual harassment on work and the psychological well-being of African-American women." *Journal of Occupational Health Psychology*, 13, 137–51.

Cortina, Lilia M., Vicki J. Magley, Jill H. Williams, and Regina D. Langhout. "Incivility in the workplace: Incidence and impact." *Journal of Occupational Health Psychology* 6, 64–80.

Fitzgerald, Louise F., Suzanne Swan, and Karla Fischer. 1995. "Why didn't she just report him? The psychological and legal implications of women's responses to sexual harassment." *Journal of Social Issues* 51, 117–38.

Gutek, Barbara. 1985. *Sex and the Workplace*. San Francisco, CA: Jossey-Bass.

Gutek, Barbara. 2001. "Women and paid work." *Psychology of Women Quarterly* 25, 379–93.

Heilman, Madeline E., Aaron S. Wallen, Daniella Fuchs, and Melinda M. Tamkins. 2004. "Penalties for success: Reactions to women who succeed at male gender-typed tasks." *Journal of Applied Psychology* 89, 416–27.

Icenogle, Marjorie L., Bruce W. Eagle, Sohel Ahmad, and Lisa A. Hanks. 2002. "Assessing perceptions of sexual harassment behaviors in a manufacturing environment." *Journal of Business and Psychology* 16, 601–16.

Kolbert, Elizabeth. 1991. "The Thomas nomination: Sexual harassment at work is pervasive, survey suggests." *New York Times*, October 11. http://www.nytimes.com/1991/10/11/us/the-thomas-nomination-sexual-harassment-at-work-is-pervasive-survey-suggests.html?scp=45&sq=anitapercent20hill&st=nyt&pagewanted=2

Lim, Sandy, and Lilia. M. Cortina, 2005. "Interpersonal mistreatment in the workplace: The interface and impact of general incivility and sexual harassment." *Journal of Applied Psychology* 90, 483–96.

Martell, Richard F., David M. Lane, and Cynthia Emrich. 1996. "Male-female differences: A computer simulation." *American Psychologist*, 51, 157–58.

McDonald, Paula. 2012. "Workplace sexual harassment 30 years on: A review of the literature." *International Journal of Management Reviews* 14, 1–17.

Newman, Meredith A., Roberts A. Jackson, and Douglas D. Baker. 2003. "Sexual harassment in the federal workplace." *Public Administration Review* 63, 472–83.

O'Leary-Kelly, Anne M., Lynn Bowes-Sperry, Collette A. Bates, and Emily R. Lean. 2009. "Sexual harassment at work: A decade (plus) of progress." *Journal of Management* 35, 503–36.

Rospenda, Kathleen M., Judith A. Richman, and Candice A. Shannon. 2009. "Prevalence and mental health correlates of harassment of discrimination in the workplace: Results from a national study." *Journal of Interpersonal Violence* 24, 819–43.

Rudman, Laurie A., Corinne A. Moss-Racusin, Julie F. Phelan, and Sanne Nauts. 2011. "Status incongruity and backlash effects: Defending the gender hierarchy motivates prejudice against female leaders." *Journal of Experimental Social Psychology* 48, 165–79.

Rudman, Laurie A., and Julie E. Phelan. 2008. "Backlash effects for disconfirming gender stereotypes in organizations." *Research in Organizational Behavior* 28, 61–79.

Valian, Virginia. 1998. *Why So Slow? The Advancement of Women*. Cambridge, MA: MIT Press.

Willness, Chelsea R., Piers Steel, and Kibeom Lee. 2007. "A meta-analysis of the antecedents and consequences of workplace sexual harassment." *Personnel Psychology* 60, 127–62.

SUPREMACY CRIMES

GLORIA STEINEM

I learned a saying from feminists in Indian Country: "The root of oppression is the loss of memory."[1]

That has special meaning in this land where we're just learning that feminism *is* memory. The cultures here, before Europeans showed up, were cultures of balance that inspired the suffrage movement—but the saying also has meaning in all of our lives.

What we can do to help each other—and for justice—is to restore, supplement, and extend each other's memories. For instance, no one person really knew all the details of the Anita Hill and Clarence Thomas hearings before the Senate Judiciary Committee, yet many of us have details to contribute to the whole picture.

1. Paula Gunn Allen, an American Indian scholar and poet, wrote this sentence in *The Sacred Hoop: Recovering the Feminine in American Indian Traditions*. As she explained there: "Beliefs, attitudes, and laws [such as those within the six nations of the Iroquois Confederacy] became part of the vision of American feminists and of other human liberation movements around the world. Yet feminists too often believe that no one has ever experienced the kind of society that empowered women and made that empowerment the basis of its rules and civilization. The price the feminist community must pay because it is not aware of the recent presence of gynarchical societies on this continent is necessary confusion, division, and much lost time."

I know Senator Arlen Specter was shocked at the amount of opposition he got from women all over the country after he attacked Anita Hill repeatedly during those hearings. As a pro-choice Republican, he had imagined he was safe in some way. I didn't know him, but he happened to cross my path, and he actually appealed to me about what he should do. I said, "You should get up and apologize in public. In the same way the cure has to address the disease, your apology has to be as public as the horrendous false accusations."

To my knowledge, he never apologized. Perhaps he should have—as has been said, "It troubles us when there is no justice."

Other things to remember: sexual harassment was first named at a 1975 speak-out held at the Women's Center at Cornell University. Students were reporting what had happened to them in summer jobs, and that was the chosen name.

It was Paulette Barnes who brought the first sexual harassment case under Title VII of the Civil Rights Act of 1964; an act in which gender was included almost as a joke.

It was Mechelle Vinson, whose case of being raped by her supervisor for two-and-a-half years—and keeping quiet in order to keep her job—caused the Supreme Court to rule in 1986 that this was sex discrimination.

I hope we notice that, with Anita Hill, these three great pioneers of protesting sexual harassment were all women of color, all African American women. I hope we might rethink our easy definition of the second wave as mostly "white and middle class;" a definition that renders invisible all the women of color who were in the leadership of this movement.

It was the clear legal mind of Catharine MacKinnon, a European American woman, that defined and wrote the textbook on sexual harassment as sex discrimination.

It's because of these four strong voices that a new immigrant in New York, working as a hotel housekeeper, knew she had a right to bodily integrity. Because she had the courage to come forward against sexual harassment by Dominique Strauss-Kahn, a woman in another country did the same. Both lost in the courts—the legal redress that was available to them—but both won in the court of public opinion. The housekeeper won because other women came forward and said what had happened to them. She won in much shorter order than the unfair number of years that Anita Hill has had to spend before she was believed, honored, and trusted by the majority of people in this country. That's why Clarence Thomas is on the Supreme Court. But Strauss-Kahn is never going to be president of France.

I learned feminism disproportionately from women of color. It was the National Welfare Rights Organization that did a brilliant analysis of the welfare system as a gigantic husband that was jealous and looked under your bed for the shoes of other men. That was the first true feminist analysis of social policy that I'd ever heard. It was my speaking partner Florynce Kennedy and her verbal karate—after which I was such an anticlimax that I always had to speak before her. It was Eleanor Holmes Norton—and so many more. It is by example that each of us learns and leads. It's how we behave, who we know, what we say. It's how we characterize the movement, whether we are in academia or in the media, that is taken to be accurate by those around us.

But there are still frontiers of things that we *don't* know. For instance, take the US military, which happens to be the largest managed economy in the world. Suppose you were a woman in the military who was fighting or training next to an eighteen-or twenty-five-year-old Clarence Thomas or Strauss-Kahn—who has a gun and perhaps is your commanding officer. That's what is faced by women in the military.

In 2010, the Department of Defense estimated that only 13 percent of survivors of sexual assault in the military reported those assaults, and only 20 percent of those cases went to trial. Of those cases, only 53 percent of the harassers, assaulters, or rapists were convicted.

Most of the women and a third of the men—because some men are also sexually assaulted—report that the sexual aggressor stalked them for a long period of time prior to the assault. They were living with fear and tension in close quarters, not just eight hours a day, but twenty-four hours a day.

Sexual assault is the leading cause of posttraumatic stress among women veterans. It results in depression, stress and high rates of substance abuse. Female rape, sexual assault and harassment survivors report a lower satisfaction rate—to put it mildly—with the Veterans' Health Services. Just treating sexual assault within the military costs $800 million a year in tax dollars.

But I'm hopeful because, for instance, SWAN, the Service Women's Action Network, is a group that represents women veterans returning from all wars, and employs all types of healing tactics. For all of us, women in the military are a frontier for questions of sexual harassment.

I submit that in the future, we will understand that all those crimes that have no reward of money or power in a real worldly sense, these crimes that have no motive except the need to prove supremacy should be called Supremacy Crimes.

That includes domestic violence, which has no reward or motive other than proving power and supremacy. It includes the so-called senseless killings by men who go into a school or a restaurant or a post office and kill people they don't know, whether it's the Montreal Massacre by a student who said he was killing feminists, or the mass murders in Norway by a man whose writings explained his hatred of women. They were all men motivated by the cult of masculinity and who said so in the ways they explained their crimes.

Yet, especially in the school killings in this country, the press tends to say, "What's happening to our children?" It is not our children. The perpetrators of those crimes were one hundred percent male, one hundred percent white, and one hundred percent non-poor. They were men who through no fault of theirs, got born into a system that told them they—by those categories of sex and race and class—have a right to control other people. It is those people who become so addicted to power and superiority that against their own short-term and long-term interests, they go into a public space and kill others.

I think about an addiction to control and supremacy when I look at the ultra right-wing in this country. They also have been born into a structure that made them believe in a birthright of control. Yet now, this country is slipping out of their control. As a result, there are more guns being bought—even just counting those bought with permits. More people are joining racist groups and ultra right-wing groups. There is more virulent and violent rhetoric in our political life. There is more legislation against everything to do with women's reproductive freedom.

Why? Because we have turned against two wars much faster then we turned against Vietnam. We will soon no longer be a majority European American, a majority white country. We have a proud African American family in the White House. We are critical of our financial institutions in a way that we never have been before.

The paradigm of all violence is what happens in the family. The time of maximum danger for a woman in a violent household is the moment just *before* she escapes or just *after* she escapes. It is then that she is most likely to be seriously injured or murdered—because she is escaping control.

Now, we are facing this in a larger sense, because the country is escaping control. Therefore, those whose identity rests on control are in full backlash.

But just as we would never advise a woman to stay in a violent home, we in this country are not going to stop becoming free. There are two things we need to understand. There is never just one alternative; there are sometimes many and always at least two things we can do. First, we must protect each other. We are living in a time of danger. Second, we must know in our hearts that we are about to be free—and we will not stop.

Those two truths will help us, whether we look at the microcosm of sexual harassment as a crime of supremacy and control, or whether we look at the political situation as a backlash from those who are accustomed to supremacy and control.

But the surge toward democracy is viewed as dangerous only by the few. We have the strength to go forward to individuality, uniqueness, community, and freedom.

GLORIA STEINEM is a writer, lecturer, editor, and feminist activist. She is particularly interested in the shared origins of sex and race caste systems, gender roles and child abuse as roots of violence, nonviolent conflict resolution, the cultures of indigenous peoples, and organizing across boundaries for peace and justice. In 1968, she helped to found *New York* magazine, where she was a political columnist and wrote feature articles. In 1972, she co-founded *Ms.* magazine, and remained one of its editors for fifteen years. She has produced a documentary on child abuse for HBO, a feature film about the death penalty for Lifetime, and has been the subject of profiles on Lifetime and HBO. Her books include the best sellers *Revolution from Within: A Book of Self-Esteem*, *Outrageous Acts and Everyday Rebellions*, *Moving Beyond Words*, and *Marilyn: Norma Jean*, on the life of Marilyn Monroe. Steinem helped to found many organizations, including the National Women's Political Caucus, Voters for Choice, the Ms. Foundation for Women, and the Women's Media Center.

VERY EASY TO SAY AND VERY HARD TO DO–
EVEN TWENTY YEARS LATER

DEVON W. CARBADO

There is so much to say as we mark the twentieth anniversary of the Anita Hill-Clarence Thomas hearings. Perhaps not surprisingly, many people have been asking some variation on the question, "What have we learned?" While this is an enormously important question to ask, it elides a more difficult one that we should put on the table as well: What should we have known, or at least surmised, about the kind of jurisprudence Clarence Thomas would write? The short answer is that we should have understood that, from a progressive perspective, Clarence Thomas presented us with an intersectional problem. That is to say, we should have known that the trajectory of Thomas's jurisprudence was going to be conservatively marked not only with respect to gender and sexuality, but also with respect to race. My hope is that, going forward, we will understand this, and that we will embrace and articulate an intersectionality-oriented politics, and that this politics will reflect a deep commitment to both feminism and antiracism.

But that is very easy to say and very hard to do—even twenty years later. This might explain the dearth of feminist engagements of Clarence Thomas's racial jurisprudence and the absence of racial critiques of his gender case law. Twenty years later, the problem Clarence Thomas presents for progressive civil rights reform remains to be articulated in intersectional terms. Such an intersectional analysis is crucial against the background of the hearings themselves. Part of the difficulty Anita Hill faced in the context of trying to tell her story related to her credibility. Her problem wasn't simply that she is a woman and that women are not believed when they allege sexual harassment. Her problem, more specifically, was that she is a black woman and black women in particular are not believed when they allege gender violence.

The issue was further complicated because Clarence Thomas is a black man. His intersectional identity as black and male vis-à-vis a black woman's claim of sexual harassment is precisely what gave him currency in the context of the hearings. When Thomas referred to the proceedings as a "high-tech lynching" he solidified his status as a racial victim. There was no trope upon which Anita Hill could call upon to perform similar ideological work. Thus, many in the black community did not perceive her to be a racial victim at all. Indeed, at least some discourses effectively described Hill as a "race traitor"—a black woman who was helping a predominately white male institution (the Senate) to "bring down" a black man. As we engage in this act of collective remembrance, we shouldn't forget this intraracial piece of the Anita Hill-Clarence Thomas moment. We need to remember that many in the black community were critical of Anita Hill or slow to support her. Moreover, when civil rights leaders (finally) raised questions about whether Clarence Thomas's jurisprudence would be damaging to civil rights and the African American community specifically, virtually none of those questions were framed in terms of gender.

White feminist interventions with respect to race were no

better. They did not highlight, for example, how sexual harassment itself is racialized, notwithstanding that the person standing in for the problem—Anita Hill—is black. The racial dimensions of her experience were largely erased, as was the racialized context in which sexual harassment law emerged. Finally, there was very little discussion among white feminists about what Clarence Thomas's racial jurisprudence might look like. The focus was ostensibly on gender per se.

Of course, there is nothing inherently wrong with framing sexual harassment in terms of gender vulnerability. The problem is that, in the context of the hearings, this "just gender" frame—which historically has privileged the experiences of white women—obfuscated important racial dynamics, only some of which I have discussed here, and precluded a conversation about whether and to what extent Clarence Thomas's jurisprudence was likely undermine the civil rights of racially marginalized groups.

This should trouble us. Clarence Thomas's racial jurisprudence has been decidedly problematic—and in ways that we could have at least partially anticipated. Roughly, the narrative that underwrites his case law is that racial consciousness is per se bad; taking race into account is per se bad; paying attention to race is per se bad. What this means for Justice Thomas, concretely, is that we should think about racial remediation in the same way we think about Jim Crow. Both are normatively pernicious because both are predicated on the idea that race matters.

Justice Thomas's views about race are part of a broader body of conservative case law whose doctrinal analysis is built upon the claim that the government should not be permitted to (1) implement affirmative action programs (because racial consciousness led to the internment of Japanese Americans during World War

II), (2) create majority/minority voting districts (because that kind of racial consciousness approximates the apartheid regime that structured South African society), and (3) engage in desegregation efforts (because that kind of racial consciousness led to the Jim Crow laws that *Brown v. Board of Education* helped to dismantle).

Conflating various forms of racial consciousness in this way is both ideologically convenient and simplistic. Who *really* believes that the creation of majority/minority voting districts as a remedial response to the history of de jure racial discrimination in voting, current racialized block voting, and the underrepresentation of nonwhites in various political offices is an iteration of South African apartheid? And even if one disagrees with affirmative programs, who *really* believes that they are analogous to the measures the government employed to intern Japanese Americans or to the "separate but equal" laws that defined the Jim Crow era? It's fair to say that most people don't *really* believe that these comparisons descriptively work. Yet, the comparisons—almost literally as I have presented them—continue to occupy legitimate space in Thomas's jurisprudence and the jurisprudence of his conservative colleagues.

None of this is to say that Justice Thomas is merely a clone of the other conservative justices on the court. He is not. He has his own voice. He speaks in that voice. And it is a voice that is decidedly racialized. Not only does Clarence Thomas vociferously argue against what he perceives to be racial paternalism, but he does so by invoking black civil rights icons, such as Frederick Douglass. In this respect, Justice Thomas trades on the very thing in which he disavows having an investment—race. This is an argument that Cheryl Harris and I make in an article in the *California Law Review* called, "The New Racial Preferences." As an example of what we mean when we say that Justice Thomas is invested in racial consciousness, notwithstanding his disavowal, consider *United States v. Fordice.*

In *Fordice* the Supreme Court explored the constitutionality of desegregation mandates in higher education. More specifically, the Court had to navigate the tension between dismantling a dual system (i.e., one in which whites and blacks are formally racially segregated) and the existence of historically black colleges and universities. Thomas begins his concurrence in that case with a quotation from W. E. B. DuBois: "We must rally to the defense of our schools. We must repudiate this unbearable assumption of the right to kill institutions unless they conform to one narrow standard." Significantly, Thomas is part of the "we" in DuBois's quote. Moreover, he is trading on that racial association. One would not expect to find DuBois in the jurisprudence of Justices Scalia or Rehnquist.

Similarly in *Missouri v. Jenkins,* a case in which a lower court had ordered the school district to make major financial investments to address inequalities under the idea of increasing "desegregative attractiveness," Thomas, along with the majority, struck down the remedial measures and declared the Kansas City school system to be unitary. Thomas adopted this approach, notwithstanding pervasive de facto segregation and inequality. More relevant for our purposes, he denounced the lower court's intervention, stating, "It never ceases to amaze me that the courts are so willing to assume that anything that is predominately black must be inferior." In these and other cases Thomas either implicitly or explicitly marks himself as black, or draws upon black culture, history, or intellectual traditions, to argue for colorblindness.

What would a feminist critique of Thomas's racial jurisprudence look like? How do feminists understand this jurisprudence against the backdrop of the hearings? What does this body of case law tell us about intersectionality? Twenty years later these questions are still largely unanswered.

Nor do we have answers to what Clarence Thomas's gender jurisprudence portends vis-à-vis antiracist organizing. Justice Thomas has limited the rights of victims of gender violence to sue for damages, formulated a thin conception of sexual harassment, situated himself on the wrong side of the Supreme Court's jurisprudence on sexual orientation, and argued against a woman's right to choose. Indeed, with respect to the last item, Justice Thomas has described *Roe v. Wade* as "grievously wrong."

What would a racial critique of this gender jurisprudence look like? How do antiracist advocates understand this jurisprudence against the backdrop of the hearings? What does this body of case law tell us about intersectionality? Twenty years later these questions are still largely unanswered.

What I am trying to suggest, in short, is that we have to begin taking intersectionality more seriously. It's not some buzzword that we can simply invoke. It's a political practice, something we must do. We didn't do intersectionality very well twenty years ago. I want to believe that we can do better going forward. That would be one way to honor Anita Hill's courage and commitment. That would be one way to remember her struggle—and the struggle of women everywhere.

DEVON W. CARBADO is a professor of law at the University of California, Los Angeles. He has received numerous distinctions, including Professor of the Year, the Rutter Award for Excellence in Teaching, the University Distinguished Teaching Award, the Eby Award for the Art of Teaching and a Fletcher Foundation Fellowship. He is the editor of *Race Law Stories* (with Rachel Moran), *Black Men on Race, Gender and Sexuality: A Critical Reader*, and the *Collected Writings of Bayard Rustin* (with Don Weise). He is the author of *Acting White? Rethinking Race in Post-Racial America* (with Mitu Gulati). He is a former director of the Critical Race Studies Program at UCLA Law, a faculty associate of the Ralph J. Bunche Center for African American Studies, a board member of the African American Policy Forum, and a James Town Fellow.

HOW TO RUN WITH IT

JULIE ZEILINGER

Founding and running the FBomb, a blog written for and by teenage feminists, has been rewarding in innumerable ways. I think the most valuable aspect of editing the writing and comments of teenage girls and boys from all over the world has been the insight I've gained into the main obstacles my generation feels we face. On the FBomb, my peers have written about everything from personal struggles with body image to double standards to the sexist media coverage of female political candidates to sexual harassment.

In fact, I recently asked the FBomb community what they thought about sexual harassment—what their opinions were or if they had any stories to tell. Unsurprisingly, the community unanimously responded that sexual harassment is unequivocally wrong, and that we all think it's ridiculous that it still occurs in 2011. What I found interesting, however, were the stories people chose to share about their experiences with sexual harassment. Specifically, they shared stories that contained a notable lack of action. One commenter described how she was sexually solicited by an older male mentor, then made to feel guilty about refusing him. She was left wondering if he had originally taken an interest in her because he thought she was smart, or just because he might get lucky. Another commenter described how a male peer tried to take off her bathing suit during a middle school swim lesson. Neither did anything about these instances, but admitted they felt horrible about them.

So why, even when we know it's wrong, do girls still fail to act against sexual harassment? Why don't we do something about it? Why don't we speak out against it?

There are probably countless reasons why many girls remain silent—reasons that vary greatly depending on the individual. But, overall, I think there are a few main reasons why girls today still endure sexual harassment. First, we need to look at the gender conditioning we still impose on young children. Despite decades of feminist action, despite the strides we've made, my generation was raised with gender stereotypes firmly intact. We grew up with a social structure that encourages boys to pursue girls and girls to chastely refuse. While my generation, the so-called "hook-up generation," may find ways around this—girls my age may acceptably pursue boys and our definitions of relationships may have changed—this archaic structure is still our baseline. It is the guideline we must ultimately revert to. And that is incredibly problematic.

The bottom line is boys still believe that they have an inherent entitlement. Many boys still feel that they are allowed to say whatever they want to girls and solicit them in any way they see fit. How else could a group of Yale frat boys march around their campus last year chanting, "No means yes and yes means anal"?

This gender conditioning doesn't just affect boys, though. There is still a large percentage of young women who take these comments as compliments, who see these predatory actions as flattering attention. Because, just as guys are trained to pursue women, girls are still told that our main role is to attract men. We're taught to compete with our peers for attention, and accept any and all attention we get.

Even if we reject such harassment, even if we stand up against it, the fact is that we still live in a victim-blaming culture. Consider some of the major news headlines of the past year alone. A police officer in Toronto told members of my generation that what we wear determines whether or not we will be raped. When reading the *New York Times* coverage of the gang rape of an eleven-year-old in Cleveland, Texas, the reporter quoted her neighbors as saying she wore makeup and dressed inappropriately. Our generation is paying attention—we are internalizing this. And this is evident in even the most superficial aspects of our lives. When girls my age heard that pop singer Rihanna was physically assaulted by her boyfriend, singer Chris Brown, many asked, "What did she do to force him to hit her?"

We still look at claims of sexual harassment and immediately doubt the woman. We think any woman who claims she was sexually harassed is likely overreacting, or the whole thing was probably her fault. We blame the victim because that is what credible people, like police officers, and credible news sources do. So why wouldn't we?

Another significant problem my generation faces with sexual harassment is that we're still not sure exactly what it is, and I think this stems from to our attitudes toward the feminist movement at large.

For my peers and me, feminism is no longer a fight against obvious obstacles. We won *Roe v. Wade*. We won Title IX. The list goes on. Feminism for my generation, for the most part, is not about "getting" rights. It's about preserving them. Feminism for us has largely become a much more subtle fight, full of nuance. This is where it becomes complicated for my generation to integrate our feminist beliefs and values into our daily lives. While my generation as a whole may be passionate about fighting injustices, while we may theoretically be able to identify what is acceptable and what is not, we don't recognize within the contexts of our own lives the same injustices that we speak against on a theoretical level. We have a semblance of understanding, a superficial acknowledgment of right and wrong. But it doesn't always permeate our actions. And I think our relationship with sexual harassment is a perfect example of this paradox.

As a whole, young women undeniably reject sexual harassment: we know that it is wrong and is something that should be fought. I think a lot of this understanding is a direct result of Anita Hill's courageous decision to publicly fight against sexual harassment. She did so when many of us were very young or, as in my case, before we were born. But even though we didn't witness her actions firsthand, they impacted our lives. Because of Anita Hill, we were born into an environment in which sexual harassment is taken seriously, in which it is legally considered an unacceptable offense.

Like other forms of sexism, sexual harassment in real life doesn't always have a huge flashing arrow pointing itself out to us. And yet, we expect that it will. We expect that sexual harassment will always take the form of a man physically grabbing us on the street. We think sexual harassment is our boss demanding that we sleep with him if we want to keep our jobs. We don't think of sexual harassment as uncomfortable come-ons. We don't think of sexual harassment as comments made to us on the street. We don't think of sexual harassment as the jokes guys in our classes sometimes make. And yet it is.

Whereas many offices and workplaces routinely have seminars and workshops about sexual harassment, the same does not occur in high schools, or even in middle schools. Our exposure to the concept of sexual harassment is largely delivered to us through the media. Most often, it is presented as humor. It is made fun of and it is belittled. And this is how the line can get blurred—this is how we can experience sexual harassment but feel unsure about whether or not we really did, or what to do about it.

Basically, there's a disconnect between the message that sexual harassment is wrong, and the understanding necessary to integrate this principle into our own lives. We know sexual harassment is bad, but we don't always know what to do when the hypothetical becomes real. There are many young women who are taking action, who are speaking out against sexual harassment, and refusing to tolerate it any longer. I think this is evident from the recent SlutWalks, in which young women marched in the street protesting our victim-blaming culture. I think this is evident from Hollaback, an organization started by young women that encourages other women to post pictures of the men who sexually harass us online, and therefore hold them accountable for their actions.

I think this is evident from recent legal cases, in which young women did fight sexual harassment. In *Simpson v. University of Colorado Boulder*, female university students brought charges against fellow male university students who sexually harassed and assaulted them at a party and held the university accountable for their past indifference about such matters. We also recently witnessed the case of *Jennings v. University of North Carolina*, in which a female university soccer player brought charges against her coach, who sexually harassed her and her fellow teammates. Those young women recognized an injustice and took action.

It's not that there is no hope left for my generation. It's just that our work isn't yet done. And believe me, there are plenty of us who are willing to continue the fight, to take Anita Hill's legacy, and run with it.

JULIE ZEILINGER, from Pepper Pike, Ohio, is a member of the Barnard College class of 2015, and is the founder and editor of *The FBomb* (thefbomb.org), a feminist blog and community for young adults who care about their rights and want to be heard. *The FBomb* posts articles of teenage and college-age feminists from all over the world about issues such as pop culture and self-image, while also promoting open dialogue about issues like politics and social justice. She is also the author of *A Little F'd Up: Why Feminism Is Not A Dirty Word.*

THE SCARLET C

LYNN NOTTAGE

A spoken remembrance.

It's senior year. A large public high school in Harlem, passes as ethnically diverse, which in 1982 means it's black and Latino with a requisite sprinkling of white students from the outer boroughs and lower Manhattan.

I am in an advanced English class, and the room looks decidedly different from the rest of the school. It is suburban in complexion, thus predominately white. I'm one of a handful of black students in the classroom, and I am beyond thrilled to be there; my hard work has paid off and I bask in my own private sense of accomplishment. Advanced English is the gateway to a good college, and I know that only a few of us—minorities— are allowed entry into the class.

It's second period. We sit alphabetically, so I am seated right smack in the center of the room. You can't miss me; I am still wearing an enormous Afro, though it's been out of fashion for nearly six years and won't come back into fashion for another fifteen. Nevertheless, I wear my Afro with a mystifying sense of confidence. This is all to say that my presence is such that I can't easily be ignored.

The teacher is an attractive white woman, a brunette with long wispy hair carelessly pulled back into an uncommitted bun at the back of her head. Her style is borrowed from Annie Hall, and she holds an invisible wand between her fingers that she waves in the air when making a salient point. We all believe her to be a great intellectual because she quotes from Sylvia Plath and T.S. Eliot.

It is my turn. I read a paragraph from The Scarlet Letter, aloud. I have all of one minute to assert my presence before disappearing back into my dark hole at the center of the classroom. I read with passion; my voice is clarion and theatrical. It is one of the few moments I get to shine. I read with such conviction that I halfway expect applause when I finish. But, there is none. In fact, there is no acknowledgment at all, instead the teacher glides her bony finger down the attendance roll and calls out the name of the boy seated in front of me. He's a disheveled white boy, who at the age of sixteen has already declared himself a poet. He annoys me. I am annoyed by the black sketchbook that he carries tucked beneath his arm. I am annoyed by the navy blue beret that he wears cocked to the side. I am annoyed by the way everyone sits at attention when he reads aloud. He annoys me, because his presence negates my own.

It's two months into the school year, and despite my gallant efforts to be recognized I remain invisible. But, twice a month we are asked to write a story, and I see it as my one opportunity to be noticed. I am a storyteller. So, when we get our assignment to write a short story in the voice of Hester Prynne, I embrace the task wholeheartedly. I spend the entire night conjuring Hester's voice. I actually shed real tears during the process, and when I finish I know that I've created something singular, something akin to art.

In class, I read my story aloud. I am Hester Prynne, the proud persecuted woman. I await praise. There is none. It is reserved for the scruffy poet seated in front of me. When our stories are handed back, instead of an A, I receive a big fat scarlet C. The comments are dismissive. I cry inside. It is what Hester would do. I betray none of the disappoint or self-loathing that's simmering within. I remain stoic.

And over the course of the next few months, I write more heartfelt and elaborately rendered stories. I am determined to be recognized. I try my damnedest to write bold and imaginative papers, but still I can do no better than a scarlet C. I begin to question whether I belong in the advanced English class. I feel my dream of a prestigious college drifting away in a sea of red magic marker.

But then in the middle of the school year, the teacher quite inexplicably announces a grand experiment. She asks us to write stories in the voice of authors that we've read during the course of the school year. The stories are designed to be anonymous, unsigned. She wants us to write freely, unencumbered by expectations; it is an exercise meant to liberate. I go home; the words come easily. I am Jane Eyre. I loosen my corset. I am freed by the thought that if I fail no one will know.

Second period. I slide my story into an envelope on the teacher's desk and take my seat. One by one, she reads our work aloud. When she gets to mine, I slide down in my chair. I want to hide, suddenly vulnerable and self-conscious, fully aware that I carry the scarlet C. She begins. My words tumble awkwardly from her mouth. And then something rather wonderful happens;

a smile erupts without warning. She's smiling. She appears to like my dark gothic tale. And. Another day. Second period. I slip my story into the envelope. The teacher reads it aloud. This time she stifles a giggle at the end; she likes it. I celebrate inside. And. Another day. Second period. The teacher reads my third anonymous story aloud. This time she wipes tears from her cheek with her sleeve, embarrassed by the unexpected emotions. And a small part of me is resurrected.

At the end of the semester we are finally allowed to collect our anonymous stories from an overstuffed envelope on the teacher's desk. I hunt through the pile of papers for my work, and what I discover shocks me. At the top of each of my stories rests a glorious A plus. Adrenaline. My heart screams, but I share this victory with no one.

Finally, the last week of school. Teacher's conference. There she is, baggy white shirt, fitted black vest and floor length skirt. She tells me that I've struggled with my personal voice throughout the semester; my writing was always interesting, but never fully realized. She tells me that I'm going to receive a generous seventy-five for the class, primarily because my class participation was good even if my writing was not. I am devastated. I start to leave, and then remember something. I still have my anonymous papers stuffed in my notebook. I consider, then gently place them on my teacher's desk, and alchemize all of my frustration into a bit of courage. I say, " I don't deserve a seventy-five." She begs to differ. She reiterates why I am receiving a seventy-five. The condescension is more than I can tolerate. My hand trembles, I feel anger threatening the calm in my voice, and I say, "Are you aware that all of my anonymous papers received an A plus? I find it interesting that when the papers bear my name I'm a C student, and when they don't, I am an A plus student. I leave it up to you to decide what grade I deserve, but I thought you should know." I don't call her a racist, though it's implied. I don't show my anger, thought it's abundant. I allow her actions to speak loudly and clearly for me.

And just so you know, on my report card I received a whooping ninety-five for advanced English. I often wonder how my life would be different if I had chosen to accept my fate without a fight. I wonder, how many times have I accepted that C, knowing that I deserved an A? I often wonder how many times in my life I've chosen to walk out of the room without turning back to fight. And so I share this memory in praise of Anita Hill, and all of those unheralded moments when we women, black women, found the courage and conviction to speak out against injustice.

LYNN NOTTAGE is a playwright from Brooklyn. Her plays include *Intimate Apparel*; *Fabulation, or the Re-Education of Undine*; *Crumbs from the Table of Joy*; *Las Meninas*; and *Ruined*. They have been produced and developed at theaters both nationally and internationally. She is the recipient of numerous awards, including the 2007 MacArthur Genius Award, an OBIE Award for playwriting, NY Drama Critics Circle Award, John Gassner Outer Critics Circle awards, American Theatre Critics/ Steinberg 2004 New Play Award, 2004 Francesca Primus Award, and two AUDELCO awards. Her most recent publications include *Intimate Apparel* and *Fabulation* and an anthology of her plays, *Crumbs from the Table of Joy and Other Plays*.

AFTERWORD

I was just a few months out of college and settling into my first real job when Anita Hill testified before the Senate. Throughout my undergraduate work as a women's studies major, my mother and I often talked about feminism and activism. I was very moved by a special camaraderie we developed, sharing our mutual outrage over and experiences with sexism, misogyny, patriarchy. I vividly remember discussing the Hill-Thomas hearings with her, reflecting on the price and impact of a woman speaking truth to power. We were inspired, frightened, infuriated, and emboldened all at once.

Over twenty years later, I had the great fortune to work with the phenomenal array of feminist scholars, activists, artists, and leaders who gathered to honor and reflect on the historic imprint of the incomparable Anita Hill. It is my hope that the conference we created in October 2011, and this volume which grew from it, will inspire generations of like-minded, visionary rabble-rousers, who will help us achieve freedom, equality, liberation, and justice for women everywhere—in the workplace and far beyond.

Anita Hill and the work of all the women and men in this volume play a considerable part in that struggle. I am confident that among those who gathered with us that day at Hunter College, and those of you reading this book, are the leaders who will chart the next chapters of women's empowerment and achievement—whether in the academy or the body politic, in the media, the arts, or the world we navigate every day in our homes and on our streets. They—YOU, for you are one of them—will blaze the next paths.

In the midst of recent debate on a bill that would ban abortions, Representative Lisa Brown was evicted from the Michigan state legislature for saying the word vagina. All these years after Anita Hill's brave testimony, women's speech, experiences, and bodies are still deviant, destabilizing, censured. In the public outcry that ensued, one of my favorite images from the demonstrations was of a woman carrying a simple sign: "I didn't come from your rib, you came from my vagina."

Bold truth telling and speaking out about everyday and outrageous acts of silencing—like that simple sign, like Anita's own testimony—is vital in continuing the fight for women's and gender equality, whether in the halls of government or in our own backyards. This is the same spirit that the conference lifted up, that this book carries forward.

What will you speak up about? What truth will you crack open and reveal? What will *you* change?

—Cynthia Greenberg

APPENDIX

ADDITIONAL EXCERPTS FROM THE TESTIMONY OF ANITA HILL AT THE CLARENCE THOMAS SENATE CONFIRMATION HEARINGS, OCTOBER 11, 1991

"Mr. Chairman, Senator Thurmond, members of the committee, my name is Anita F. Hill, and I am a professor of law at the University of Oklahoma. . . . I graduated from the university with academic honors and proceeded to the Yale Law School, where I received my JD degree in 1980.

Upon graduation from law school, I became a practicing lawyer with the Washington, DC, firm of Wald, Harkrader & Ross. In 1981, I was introduced to now Judge Thomas by a mutual friend. Judge Thomas told me that he was anticipating a political appointment and asked if I would be interested in working with him. He was, in fact, appointed as Assistant Secretary of Education for Civil Rights. After he had taken that post, he asked if I would become his assistant and I accepted that position.

In my early period there, I had two major projects. First was an article I wrote for Judge Thomas' signature on the education of minority students. The second was the organization of a seminar on high-risk students, which was abandoned, because Judge Thomas transferred to the EEOC, here he became the Chairman of that office.

During this period at the Department of Education, my

working relationship with Judge Thomas was positive. I had a good deal of responsibility and independence. I thought he respected my work and that he trusted my judgment.

After approximately 3 months of working there, he asked me to go out socially with him. What happened next and telling the world about it are the two most difficult things, experiences of my life. It is only after a great deal of agonizing consideration and a number of sleepless nights that I am able to talk of these unpleasant matters to anyone but my close friends.

I declined the invitation to go out socially with him, and explained to him that I thought it would jeopardize what at the time I considered to be a very good working relationship. I had a normal social life with other men outside of the office. I believed then, as now, that having a social relationship with a person who was supervising my work would be ill advised. I was very uncomfortable with the idea and told him so.

I thought that by saying "no" and explaining my reasons, my employer would abandon his social suggestions. However, to my regret, in the following few weeks he continued to ask me out on several occasions. He pressed me to justify my reasons for saying "no" to him. These incidents took place in his office or mine. They were in the form of private conversations, which would not have been overheard by anyone else.

My working relationship became even more strained when Judge Thomas began to use work situations to discuss sex. On these occasions, he would call me into his office for reports on education issues and projects or he might suggest that because of the time pressures of his schedule, we go to lunch to a government cafeteria. After a brief discussion of work, he would turn the conversation to a discussion of sexual matters. His conversations were very vivid.

He spoke about acts that he had seen in pornographic films involving such matters as women having sex with animals, and films showing group sex or rape scenes. He talked about pornographic materials depicting individuals with large penises, or large-breasted individuals in various sex acts.

On several occasions Thomas told me graphically of his own sexual prowess. Because I was extremely uncomfortable talking about sex with him at all, and particularly in such a graphic way, I told him that I did not want to talk about these subjects. I would also try to change the subject to education matters or to non-sexual personal matters, such as his background or his beliefs. My efforts to change subject were rarely successful.

Throughout the period of these conversations, he also from time to time asked me for social engagements. My reaction to these conversations was to avoid them by limiting opportunities for us to engage in extended conversations. This was difficult because at the time, I was his only assistant at the Office of Education or office for Civil Rights.

During the latter part of my time at the Department of Education, the social pressures and any conversation of his offensive behavior ended. I began both to believe and hope that our working relationship could be a proper, cordial, and professional one.

When Judge Thomas was made chair of the EEOC, I needed to face the question of whether to go with him. I was asked to do so and I did. The work, itself, was interesting, and at that time, it appeared that the sexual overtures, which had so troubled me had ended.

I also faced the realistic fact that I had no alternative job. While I might have gone back to private practice, perhaps in my old firm, or at another, I was dedicated to civil rights work and my first choice was to be in that field. Moreover, at that time the

Department of Education, itself, was a dubious venture. President Reagan was seeking to abolish the entire department.

For my first months at the EEOC, where I continued to be an assistant to Judge Thomas, there were no sexual overtures However, during the fall and winter of 1982, these began again. The comments were random, and ranged from pressing me about why I didn't go out with him, to remarks about my personal appearance. I remember him saying that someday I would have to tell him the real reason that I wouldn't go out with him.

He began to show displeasure in his tone and voice and his demeanor, in his continued pressure for an explanation. He commented on what I was wearing in terms of whether it made me more or less sexually attractive. The incidents occurred in his inner office at the EEOC.

One of the oddest episodes I remember was an occasion in which Thomas was drinking a Coke in his office, he got up from the table at which we were working, went over to his desk to get the Coke, looked at the can and asked, "Who has put pubic hair on my Coke?"

On other occasions he referred to the size of his own penis as being larger than normal and he also spoke on some occasions of the pleasures he had given to women with oral sex. At this point, late 1982, I began to feel severe stress on the job. I began to be concerned that Clarence Thomas might take out his anger with me by degrading me or not giving me important assignments. I also thought that he might find an excuse for dismissing me.

In January 1983, I began looking for another job. I was handicapped because I feared that if he found out he might make it difficult for me to find other employment, and I might be dismissed, and I might be dismissed from the job I had.

Another factor that made my search more difficult was that

this was during a period of a hiring freeze in the Government. In February 1983, I was hospitalized for 5 days on an emergency basis for acute stomach pain which I attributed to stress on the Job. Once out of the hospital, I became more committed to finding other employment and sought further to minimize my contact with Thomas.

This became easier when Allyson Duncan became office director because most of my work was then funneled through her and I had contact with Clarence Thomas mostly in staff meetings.

In the spring of 1983, an opportunity to teach at Oral Roberts University opened up. I participated in a seminar, taught an afternoon session in a seminar at Oral Roberts University. The dean of the university saw me teaching and inquired as to whether I would be interested in pursuing a career in teaching, beginning at Oral Roberts University. I agreed to take the job, in large part, because of my desire to escape the pressures I felt at EEOC due to Judge Thomas.

When I informed him that I was leaving in July, I recall that his response was that now, I would no longer have an excuse for not going out with him. I told him that I still preferred not to do so. At some time after that meeting, he asked if he could take me to dinner at the end of the term.

When I declined, he assured me that the dinner was a professional courtesy only and not a social invitation. I reluctantly agreed to accept that invitation but only if it was at the very end of a working day.

On, as I recall, the last day of my employment at the EEOC in the summer of 1983, I did have dinner with Clarence Thomas. We went directly from work to a restaurant near the office. We talked about the work that I had done both at Education and at the EEOC. He told me that he was pleased with all of it except for an article and speech that I had done for him while we were at the Office of Civil Rights. Finally he made a comment that I will vividly remember. He said that if I ever told anyone of his behavior that it would ruin his career. This was not an apology, nor was it an explanation. That was his last remark about the possibility of our going out, or reference to his behavior.

In July 1983, I left the Washington, DC, area and have had minimal contacts with Judge Clarence Thomas since. I am, of course, aware from the press that some questions have been raised about conversations I had with Judge Clarence Thomas after I left the EEOC.

From 1983 until today I have seen Judge Thomas only twice. On one occasion I needed to get a reference from him and on another, he made a public appearance at Tulsa. On one occasion he called me at home and we had an inconsequential conversation. On one occasion he called me without reaching me and I returned the call without reaching him and nothing came of it. I have, at least on three occasions, been asked to act as a conduit to him for others.

It is only after a great deal of agonizing consideration that I am able to talk of these unpleasant matters to anyone, except my closest friends as I have said before. These last few days have been very trying and very hard for me, and it hasn't just been the last few days of this week. It has actually been over a month now that I have been under the strain of this issue. Telling the world is the most difficult experience of my life, but it is very close to having to live through the experience that occasioned this meeting. I may have used poor judgment early on in my relationship with this issue. I was aware, however, that telling at any point in my career could adversely affect my future career. And I did not want, early on, to build [*sic*] all the bridges to the EEOC.

As I said, I may have used poor judgment. Perhaps I should have taken angry or even militant steps, both when I was in the agency or after I had left it, but I must confess to the world that the course I took seemed the better, as well as the easier approach.

I declined any comment to newspapers, but later when Senate staff asked me about these matters, I felt that I had a duty to report. I have no personal vendetta against Clarence Thomas. I seek only to provide the committee with information, which it may regard as relevant.

It would have been more comfortable to remain silent. I took no initiative to inform anyone. But when I was asked by a representative of this committee to report my experience I felt that I had to tell the truth. I could not keep silent.

This is an excerpt from the hearings before the Committee on the Judiciary, United States Senate on the nomination of Clarence Thomas to be associate justice of the Supreme Court of the United States. It can be accessed online at http://mith .umd.edu//WomensStudies/GenderIssues/SexualHarassment/ hill-thomas-testimony.

DISCUSSION QUESTIONS ON
ANITA HILL'S TESTIMONY

1. What is your reaction to the Anita Hill's testimony?
2. If you were an adult at the time of the hearings, did you see an impact from her testimony in your life or in your workplace then or soon thereafter?
3. What lasting impact do you think her testimony has had?
4. What challenges do we still face and where can we go from here?
5. Hill said it would have been more comfortable to stay silent about her experiences, do you recall a time when you decided to speak out rather than stay silent about an injustice or difficult subject? What was the topic and what was the outcome?

TOOLKIT FOR ADDRESSING SEXUAL HARASSMENT IN THE WORKPLACE

WHAT IS SEXUAL HARASSMENT?

Sexual harassment includes severe or pervasive conduct in the workplace related to a person's sex that negatively affects a reasonable person's employment. It includes: verbal or written comments about someone's appearance or behavior; sexual jokes and innuendoes; requesting sexual favors or repeatedly asking a person out; sexual leering; following; inappropriate touching; and drawings, posters, email images, or screen savers that are sexual in nature. Unfortunately, sexual harassment is common in workplaces throughout the United States.

WHAT LAW PROHIBITS SEXUAL HARASSMENT IN THE WORKPLACE?

Sexual harassment is a form of sex discrimination that violates Title VII of the Civil Rights Act of 1964. Title VII is a federal law that prohibits discrimination in employment on the basis of sex, race, color, national origin, and religion, and it applies to employers with fifteen or more employees, including federal, state, and local governments. Title VII also applies to private and public colleges and universities, employment agencies, and labor organizations. Title VII reads:

> It shall be an unlawful employment practice for an employer (1) to fail or refuse to hire or to discharge any individual, or otherwise to discriminate against any individual with respect to his compensation, terms, conditions, or privileges of employment, because of such individual's race, color, religion, sex, or national origin; or (2) to limit, segregate, or classify his employees or applicants for employment in any way which would deprive or tend to deprive any individual of employment opportunities or otherwise adversely affect his status as an employee, because of such individual's race, color, religion, sex, or national origin.
>
> It shall be an unlawful employment practice for an employment agency to fail or refuse to refer for employment, or otherwise to discriminate against, any individual because of his race, color, religion, sex, or national origin, or to classify or refer for employment any individual on the basis of his race, color, religion, sex, or national origin.

There are two established, legally prohibited types of sexual harassment:

1. Quid pro quo: Compliance or noncompliance with a sexual demand is used as the basis of an employment decision.

2. Hostile work environment: An employee is subject to unwelcome verbal or physical sexual behavior, including requests for sexual favors and other conduct of a sexual nature that is either so severe or pervasive that it adversely affects her or his ability to do work.

Retaliation against someone who complains of sexual harassment or participates in an investigation involving sexual harassment is also illegal under Title VII of the Civil Rights Act.

WHAT IS REQUIRED OF EMPLOYERS?

Title VII makes employers liable to prevent and stop sexual harassment of employees. Under Title VII, covered employers must: (1) take reasonable care to prevent sexual harassment; (2) take reasonable care to promptly correct sexual harassment that has occurred. Before an employer can be legally responsible for taking reasonable care to correct sexual harassment, the employer must be made aware that the harassment has occurred. Employees should follow their company's internal grievance procedures, if they exist, or to otherwise notify their supervisor about the harassment.

WHAT CAN I DO IF I BELIEVE I HAVE BEEN SEXUALLY HARASSED AT WORK?

You should notify your employer or supervisor immediately. If your employer has a sexual harassment policy in place, follow it, and expect your employer to follow it as well. Put complaints in writing. Take notes on the harassment and be specific in your details—note the time and place of each incident, what was said and done, and who witnessed the actions. If your employer fails to take action, consult an attorney. Should you wish to gain more information or file a complaint, contact the EEOC. Act quickly; if you fail to act within a specific period of time, you may lose your ability to take legal action.

WHAT REMEDIES ARE AVAILABLE UNDER TITLE VII?

Important time limits apply to sex discrimination claims under Title VII. Individuals have one hundred and eighty days from the date of the last incident of discrimination to file a complaint with the Equal Employment Opportunity Commission (EEOC). This one-hundred-and-eighty-day filing deadline is extended to three hundred days if the charge also is covered by a state or local anti-discrimination law. Using internal procedures at one's workplace does not extend the time limit under federal law, although it may under some state laws. To preserve a sex discrimination claim under Title VII, contact the EEOC to find out what time limit applies. To preserve your sex discrimination claim under state law, contact the state fair employment practices agency in your state. An attorney is not necessary to file a complaint with the EEOC. Approximately fifteen thousand sexual harassment cases are brought to the EEOC each year.

WHAT WILL THE EEOC DO?

Once a charge of discrimination is filed with the EEOC, the employer will be notified that a charge of discrimination has been filed, and the EEOC will begin an investigation. The EEOC may attempt to settle the charge of discrimination or may refer the charge to its mediation program, which is a voluntary, confidential process requiring the consent of both parties. If the EEOC is unable to reach a settlement agreement, and it is a private employer, the EEOC may file a lawsuit in federal court. If the employer is a public employer, the EEOC will refer the matter for litigation to the Employment Litigation Section of the Civil Rights Division at the US Department of Justice.

The EEOC may also choose to dismiss the charge. When a charge is dismissed, or if the EEOC is unable to reach an agreement to settle the complaint after finding discrimination, the EEOC issues a notice of the individual's right to file a lawsuit on her or his own behalf within ninety days. Individuals who have filed charges with the EEOC have the right to request this notice if they wish to proceed to court and the EEOC has not completed its process.

WHAT RELIEF IS AVAILABLE IF THERE IS A FINDING OF SEX DISCRIMINATION BY THE COURT?

If there is a finding of sex discrimination, relief is intended to make the individual "whole;" in other words, to put the individual in the place she or he would have been had the discrimination not occurred. Such relief can include back pay, front pay, hiring, promotion or tenure, and reinstatement. Damages may be available to compensate for monetary losses, future monetary losses, and mental anguish and inconvenience. Punitive damages also may be available if an employer acted with malice or reckless indifference. Additional remedies may include attorney's fees, expert witness fees, and court costs.

ADDITIONAL RESOURCES

9 to 5: National Association of Working Women
www.9to5.org

American Association of University Women
www.aauw.org

American Civil Liberties Union
www.aclu.org

Equal Employment Opportunity Commission (EEOC)
File charges: www.eeoc.gov/employees/charge.cfm

Equal Rights Advocates
www.equalrights.org

Feminist Majority Foundation
www.feminist.org

Institute for Women's Policy Research
www.iwpr.org

National Organization for Women
www.now.org

National Organization for Women—NYC
www.nownyc.org

National Partnership for Women and Families
www.nationalpartnership.org

National Women's Law Center
www.nwlc.org

Rape, Abuse & Incest National Network
www.rainn.org

Service Women's Action Network
www.servicewomen.org

Sexual Harassment Support
www.sexualharassmentsupport.org

United States Department of Labor
www.dol.gov

CO-SPONSORS AND
ADDITIONAL RESOURCES

Here are the more than seventy co-sponsoring organizations that propelled the movement behind the conference, Sex, Power, and Speaking Truth: Anita Hill 20 Years Later. These organizations—from grassroots to academic to major institutions of the women's movement—represent a range of gender-related issues, and all are made up of hardworking individuals eager to see more gender equality in the world.

A Call To Men
www.acalltomen.org

A Long Walk Home
www.alongwalkhome.org

ACLU Women's Rights Project
www.aclu.org/womens-rights

American Association of University Women
www.aauw.org

Auburn Theological Seminary
www.auburnseminary.org

Barnard Center for Research on Women
bcrw.barnard.edu

Bella Abzug Leadership Institute
www.abzuginstitute.org

Black Women's Blueprint
www.blackwomensblueprint.org

Brandeis University Women's and Gender Studies Program
www.brandeis.edu/programs/wgs

Brandeis University Women's Studies Research Center
www.brandeis.edu/wsrc

Brooklyn College: Shirley Chisholm Project of Brooklyn
Women's Activism
chisholmproject.com

Brooklyn College Women's Center
depthome.brooklyn.cuny.edu/womens/center

Brooklyn College Women's Studies Program
www.brooklyn.cuny.edu/pub/departments/WomensStudies

CONNECT
www.connectnyc.org

CUNY Graduate Center: Center for the Study of Women &
Society
web.gc.cuny.edu/womencenter/index.htm

CUNY Graduate Center: CLAGS: The Center for Lesbian
and Gay Studies
web.gc.cuny.edu/clags/index.php

CUNY Graduate Program in Political Science
www.gc.cuny.edu/Academics-Research-Centers-Initiatives/
Doctoral-Programs/Political-Science

CUNY School of Law
www.law.cuny.edu

Domestic Abuse Shelter, Inc.
www.domesticabuseshelter.org/DASinformation.htm

The Eleanor Roosevelt Legacy
www.eleanorslegacy.com

Equal Rights Advocates
www.equalrights.org

Feminist.com
www.feminist.com

The Feminist Press at CUNY
www.feministpress.org

Feministing.com
www.feministing.com

GEMS: Girls Education & Mentoring Services
www.gems-girls.org

Girls for Gender Equity
www.ggenyc.org

Hedgebrook
www.hedgebrook.org

Hollaback!
www.ihollaback.org

Hunter College: The Women and Gender Studies Program
www.hunter.cuny.edu/wgsprogram

Institute for Research in African-American Studies at Columbia University
www.iraas.com

The Institute for Women's Health and Leadership: Vision 2020
Drexel University College of Medicine
www.drexel.edu/vision2020

Jack & Jill Politics
www.jackandjillpolitics.com

Jewish Women's Archive
www.jwa.org

Jews for Racial & Economic Justice
www.jfrej.org

Lehman College
www.lehman.cuny.edu

The Line Campaign
whereisyourline.org

Macaulay Honors College at CUNY
macaulay.cuny.edu

Ms. Foundation for Women
ms.foundation.org

Ms. magazine
www.msmagazine.com

My Sisters' Place
mysistersplaceny.org

The Nation
www.thenation.com

National Council for Research on Women
www.ncrw.org

National Council of Jewish Women
www.ncjw.org

National Organization for Women/NYC
www.nownyc.org

National Women's Law Center
www.nwlc.org

Outten and Golden LLP
www.outtengolden.com

Pace Law School
www.law.pace.edu

Purchase College/SUNY
www.purchase.edu

Queens College Women's Center
mysite.verizon.net/olegos

Right Rides for Women's Safety
rightrides.org

Roosevelt House Public Policy Institute at Hunter College
roosevelthouse.hunter.cuny.edu

Rutgers Labor and Employment Law Society:
Rutgers School of Law, Newark
law.newark.rutgers.edu/students/student-organizations

Service Women's Action Network
servicewomen.org

Soapbox, Inc.
www.soapboxinc.com

Stop Street Harassment
www.stopstreetharassment.org

Students Active for Ending Rape (SAFER)
www.safercampus.org

Third Wave Foundation
www.thirdwavefoundation.org

University at Albany Department of History
www.albany.edu/history

University at Albany Department of Sociology
www.albany.edu/sociology

University at Albany Division of Student Success
www.albany.edu/studentsuccess

University at Albany Department of Women's Studies
www.albany.edu/womensstudies

University of Connecticut School of Law
www.law.uconn.edu

University of Connecticut Women's Center
www.womenscenter.uconn.edu

University of Connecticut Women's Studies Program
www.womens.studies.uconn.edu

V-Day
www.vday.org/home

VOICE MALE magazine
voicemalemagazine.org

Voices of Women Organizing Project
vowbwrc.org

WET Productions
www.wetweb.org

The White House Project
www.thewhitehouseproject.org

Women's Center at John Jay College
www.jjay.cuny.edu/1974.php

Women's City Club of New York
wccny.org

Women's eNews
womensenews.org

The Women's Institute at Omega
eomega.org/omega/womensinstitute

Women's Media Center
www.womensmediacenter.com

ACKNOWLEDGMENTS

In October 2011 a tremendous and tenacious group assembled to honor Anita Hill. Held at Hunter College in New York City, Sex, Power and Speaking Truth: Anita Hill 20 Years Later commemorated twenty years since Hill's appearance before the Senate Judiciary Committee. The rigorous dialogue and generosity of spirit that made that day a success, is what inspired this collection. We extend our thanks to all who made that and this volume possible.

First and foremost, we have to thank the visionary organizing committee and its fearless co-chairs Kathleen Peratis and Letty Cottin Pogrebin. These volunteers gave their time for almost a year working to make this historic endeavor a reality: Purva Panday Cullman, Eve Ensler, Deborah Slaner Larkin, Pat Mitchell, Farah Tanis, and Patricia Williams. Amy Richards was also a member of that committee, and Cynthia Greenberg was the conference coordinator. Eve Ensler and Purva Panday Cullman of V-Day deserve extra thanks for producing and curating the beautiful and moving performance that closed the day.

We were also joined by over seventy co-sponsoring organizations; we extend special appreciation to Jennifer Raab and the leadership of Hunter College. Others helped to ensure that day was well-attended and documented, including Holly Kearl of Stop Street Harassment, who assembled a comprehensive resource guide; the co-sponsoring organizations who coordinated important break-out discussions during the day, and McKensey Smith and Agatha Paterson from Third Wave Foundation for leading the effort; the hundreds of volunteers who fueled the day, and to Farah Tanis and Cristina Jaus who organized them all. The day was well-documented thanks to photographers Carolina Kroon, Jenny Warburg, and Domenica Comfort, filmmaker Freida Mock, and designers Lili Schwartz and Ben Agronick. Peter Hart deserves thanks for his fast and furious transcription of the day.

Our special thanks to those who underwrote the costs of that day-long event and thus made that and this book possible, including: Esther-Ann Asch, Barbara Dobkin, Sunny Goldberg, Anne Hess, Hunter College, Sarah Kovner, Deborah Slaner Larkin, the Ms. Foundation for Women, Susan and Leonard Nimoy, Kathleen Peratis, Nadine Schiff and Frederic Rosen, Nancy Rubin, Deborah Sagner, the Sister Fund, SUNY Purchase/Purchase College, V-Day, Katrina vanden Heuvel, The White House Project, Barbara Whitman, and Lois Whitman.

We thank the more than two thousand people who spent October 15, 2011, at Hunter College, including all those who spoke and performed, asked questions, and spoke up. Your wit and wisdom fill the bulk of this volume as does the presence of the countless who viewed the conference via C-SPAN and CUNY TV. Among that hearty group, in attendance were Amy Scholder and Gloria Jacobs of the Feminist Press, who deserve